KIMBERLEE ANNE KING

# Parenting is hard.
# Suffering is optional.

A HANDBOOK FOR PARENTS ON THE BRINK

*Parenting is hard. Suffering is optional.*
*A Handbook for Parents on the Brink*

ISBN 978-0-9982230-0-1
Copyright © 2017 by Kimberlee Anne King
All Rights Reserved

For more information, visit www.inspiredattention.com
Book design by Tim Whitney

# Contents

Preface ..................................................... xi
Introduction ................................................ 1
Judge No More .............................................. 3
Gratitude .................................................. 15
Ego ....................................................... 19
"Where are My Fucking Cheez-its?" .......................... 27
Everything is Not Okay ..................................... 31
Why Do We Stop the Kids from Fighting? ..................... 35
The Manual ................................................ 37
Reflections ............................................... 41
Could It Be You? .......................................... 45
No, Really, the Umbilical Cord was Cut at Birth ............ 47
Being in Now .............................................. 53
Urgency ................................................... 57
The Line .................................................. 59
Feeling the Pressure to Figure out What to do Next ......... 63
Hope can be a Bitch ....................................... 67
What's in a Grade? ........................................ 73
Invisible Disabilities and Outliers ....................... 77
School Haters ............................................. 83
Clues to Reality .......................................... 87
Pluto is No Longer Labeled a Planet ....................... 93
Beautiful ................................................. 95
"Because I said so..." .................................... 97
Requests Versus Complaints ................................ 99
No Prom for Me ........................................... 105
I Don't Deserve This! .................................... 109
Really? I Have to Deal With This, Too? ................... 113
Better Off Dead .......................................... 117
The Ramen Noodle Conundrum ............................... 121
What Should We Be Teaching Our Children? ................. 127

# *Acknowledgements*

This book exists due to the influence and teachings of so many soul mates and this includes my children. I cannot possibly name all of you. For those of you who bestowed their wisdom upon me and requested nothing in return, I thank you.

**Frank Garland** - You were the one who said I would write a book. Your confidence in me and your conviction that I had something worthy of sharing was the inspiration I needed to start. You also thought I was funny. Thank you my incredibly gifted friend. The world would not be as wonderful without you.

**My Delphi University Family - Steve, Kimberly, Charles, Linda, Judy, Janice, Bruce, and Kelly (plus everyone else that makes Delphi amazing)** - You have all taught me so much. Your school is truly home for so many of us. I am grateful for all of you and the love you have shown me.

**Tim Whitney, Greenisland Media** - You have helped me navigate a very intimidating process. Your knowledge, artistic talent, and kind patience, allowed this book to actually find its way into print! Thank you so very much for all of your help in making my vision into something real.

**Rachelle Gardner** - Thank you for editing my dyslexic writing. You were able to make my writing more impactful while maintaining the meaning. And thank you for giving me the courage to move forward with the book.

**Ken** - Thank you for being dad to four of the most interesting children one could imagine! In addition to creating these children, you are a good friend. I have learned a great deal from your knowledge and diplomacy. You embrace all people from every part of the world no matter their status without judgment and are a very generous man.

**Bill and Bry (my brothers)** - I always worry about children without siblings. Who tells them the truth about how they really look or how awful their singing is? Who knows what it was really like growing up? Thank you for being my friends, playmates, and helping me grow as a person. And thank you for sharing your amazing children with me.

**Mom and Dad** - I know I was not and am not a normal child. Thank you for being my parents despite my quirky nature. I love you both and am grateful for your teachings (yes, I was paying attention).

**Ian King** - It is my opinion you are one of the most gifted people I have ever known. Your ability to see and help people, even people in the most dire of situations, is miraculous. I have learned more by watching you than I have in lifetimes of study. Thank you for your endless contributions to our book. Thank you for creating Inspired Attention with me. I hope our little company does inspire millions the courage to make conscious choice. What a world it will be!

# *Dedication*

This book is dedicated to all of my children. Thank you for teaching me, being patient with me, and loving me unconditionally. I love you all more than words can ever express.

I also dedicate this book to my husband, Ian. You are truly a gift from the Universe. You are my guide, teacher, partner, and my beacon home when I get lost in thought or emotions. This book would not exist without you. It is really our book. Your wisdom is present on every page. I am grateful for every day we have together. I love you.

*Anxiety:* Fear of the unknown. Parenthood is an orchard ripe with the fruit of the unknown.

*Learning disability:* The experience of brilliance in one's own head, behind closed doors, behind closed eyes, followed by a heart-wrenching blank piece of paper and no sound.

# Preface

I am not a natural writer. My mind is a tangent, and I will go on many during this book so please, just go with it. I'm not seeking any awards here for writing. I'm barely a reader. I have dyslexia. I have epilepsy and migraines and Ehlers-Danlos Syndrome and chronic anxiety and embarrassing social phobias that will reveal themselves in very weird ways and a bunch of other bizarre medical issues that are beyond modern medicine. I am a parent. I am a life coach and an educational consultant for gifted and learning disabled children (some children are both). I am the wife of the most amazing man I have ever met and who is my greatest teacher. I am a spiritual person. I embrace life. I love people but have very few individuals in my life with whom I am actually capable of connecting. I was a straight-A student throughout high school and graduated from the University of Iowa with honors (from the College of Business Administration in Economics if you're the curious type). I spent a semester abroad at Cambridge University. I'm pretty well traveled. I am intelligent. And, mostly, I am incredibly stubborn and refuse to allow anyone, even my own ego, tell me what I can and cannot do. (This did not go over well with my parents.)

I share this information so you might understand what my motivation is for writing and sharing this book with you. I have four challenging and unique children. I also now have three stepsons, each with their unique personalities. I have survived divorce. I have children with learning disabilities, AD/HD, anxiety, emotional problems, genetic syndromes, and issues we are still trying to figure out, let alone label. I have watched my children suffer, both emotionally and physically, some painfully so. I have searched far and wide and spent countless dollars for answers, always looking for the slightest improvement or lessening of their suffering. I amassed so much information I became a consultant for other parents struggling in the same ways. I was and still am, in moments, the go-to person for what to do next with a child at whom others point the finger (and not the nice finger) and call them "not normal." This book is a glorious celebration of my failures as a parent.

I am passionate about these children who are misfits of the systems (educational, medical, social, familial). My gift is the ability to make the complex simple. I take a really complex child who is a puzzle to most, along with a ton of information about that child, and see the path. I am told I can take complicated concepts and explain them in simple terms, and that is a relief to people. I hope I succeed with you in some fashion. If only one person benefits from my efforts, then I will have succeeded. (Between you and me, I have shared portions of this book with friends and clients and they have benefited, so the pressure is off. Yay! I hope you caught the significance in this, especially if you are a perfectionist. Perfectionism is like being an alcoholic. If you are one, you are one for life, and you need to be vigilant about supporting yourself and seeking support from others. Maybe I should start PA - Perfectionists Anonymous. Can you imagine?)

My failures have been my greatest gifts and my greatest learning. No easy thing for a perfectionist to admit. I had no handbook. (Maybe this will be your handbook.) I did wise up and eventually seek out help from enlightened, wise people who knew how to guide me.

There's the key. I needed help. My children need my love and support, and with that, they will find their way. I do not need to find answers to their problems or challenges. They need me to love them, just as they are, just as I wish to be loved just as I am, with all of my challenges and disabilities. I am completely capable of handling myself in this world. I was a fool to think my children are not equally capable.

So this book is about parenting, not about how to handle children. Parenting is about parents and how they want to handle themselves and how challenging that becomes when there are children involved, let alone children with special needs. It's painful sometimes to look into the mirror and see ourselves clearly. I wanted to write this book to help you find your best self so you can be your best self with children.

Children are our teachers. They help us see ourselves clearly, including what we cannot tolerate and what we try to minimize out of shame. I want to help you look into that mirror the children are holding up—and not freak out.

Children have a gift. They know our secrets (damn!) and know how to make us angrier than we ever thought possible. Children help us to feel fear we never expected, not even watching the scariest movie (for me that would be *The Exorcist*). They know how to push our buttons and break our hearts. In all of this, there is the answer to our greatest desire: to live a fulfilled life. Children are chaos, and the key to fulfillment is to be okay no matter what is going on in your life, no matter the chaos. My enlightened friends have had it all and then lost everything, cherished love and lost love, experienced the best and the worst life has to offer. Yet, they are grounded and clear and fulfilled. Not happy all the time—that's a myth. They are wise people. They know that the details of their chaos are irrelevant. They focus on their own responses, which is the only thing one can control amidst chaos.

Many of the moms I work with will not seek out what I will call "self care." (That is a whole other book!) They will, however, seek wisdom, which by the way includes self-care, for the sake of their children. Yes—I use it often as a manipulation in the beginning. However, very soon the mom opens her eyes and wakes up to the concept that if she is not okay, her children will not be okay. If your children are anything like mine, they need parents who are being the best version of themselves, who are tapping into their own wisdom, to help them navigate a sometimes brutally unforgiving and judgmental world.

So feel your feelings. Release your tears. Laugh. Let go of your self-judgment. Celebrate your failures. Grow. Your children are watching, and you are their greatest teacher. We all learn by watching others, and I, for one, do not want my children to be hindered by what they see in me.

# Introduction

Have you ever considered that this child—this gift from God who challenges you, who pulls relentlessly at your sanity with the persistence of the almighty termite, whom you love so deeply it frightens you, whom you tirelessly try to help—may have come into the world simply to help you grow? Ponder this for a moment. When I truly consider that my challenging and disabled children are here on Earth to serve a greater purpose, to help me find my heart, to heal my soul, to allow me to grow, I stand in awe. I am humbled. I am grateful. I feel loved. (And, in moments, I wonder what the hell I did in a past life to deserve this!)

I checked the Bible for some understanding (which is really saying something because I am not a religious person). The Bible would be so much more helpful if Christ tried to do what he did with four little kids yanking on his robes asking, "Are we there yet?" Or imagine Buddha under the Bodhi tree with a couple of toddlers needing his constant attention (or better yet, teenagers bored out of their minds constantly asking to borrow the car to drive around aimlessly for no reason). I wonder how long it would have taken for him to find enlightenment with that worry plaguing him.

Open your mind. Parenting is education at its best. We all have a lot to learn. Forgive your imperfections. If we can take on the perspective of an enthusiastic student who is learning something important, parenting will become an amazing, enlightening journey no matter what your circumstance.

CHAPTER 1

# Judge No More

If you've read all of the parenting books and in your heart you know you're a good person who loves their children, and yet you're still struggling as a parent (a.k.a. your child is not doing or behaving as you would like), take heart my friend. You are not alone. You are human, and you're looking for answers. Our society does not make this journey an easy one. What would we learn if it was?

And yet, we can begin to find answers when we consider a surprisingly simple concept. We won't find our answers in discussions of discipline tactics or empowerment strategies or the perfect way to talk to your child (although all these things are valuable). The concept is so simple that if you go quiet for a minute and consider it in your heart, you will know and feel the truth of it. The concept is, "Judge no more." Ponder it for a moment. If there could be one phrase with the power to solve most of the problems in parenting—actually, with every single relationship we have—it would be this phrase.

When we judge others, we cause pain. When we judge ourselves, we cause lots of pain. When we judge our children, we cause even more pain. But most importantly, when we judge, we step out of wisdom, for within wisdom there is no judgment. (Let's not confuse discernment or wise evaluation with judgment. If I refuse to drive 100 miles per hour over a blind hill on a dare from friends, I'm making a wise evaluation of the potential consequences.)

Judgment is thinking your way is the only way. Judgment is thinking your child is lazy. Judgment is thinking someone who looks different is less than. Judgment is calling yourself stupid for making a mistake. "I should have known better." Judgment is believing another parent is wrong in the way they are handling their children. Judgment is hatred, racism, exclusion. Sometimes, judgment is worry.

Really—worry? Isn't it our job to worry? Don't good parents worry? We can't help it. But it is critical for us to recognize when our worry stems from judgment.

I worry about my oldest son all of the time, since the day he was born. He has Ehlers-Danlos Syndrome, which took almost eighteen years of searching to figure out. He is brilliant but cannot do school very well. He can barely write, suffers from extreme, untreatable anxiety and is in pain most of the time, either physically or emotionally. He was homebound the last quarter of his junior year of high school. I worry he will never be able to care for himself. I worry he will not be able to handle college without my constant support. I worry he will decide one day he has had it and give up (and he has been there a number of times). But most of all—and this is hard to admit because it's selfish—I fear I will not be okay if he cannot find a way to walk the normal path.

You know, the normal path. The one where the kids grow up, go to school, do their homework, play sports, date, and get into trouble. And when they get into trouble you have the Mr. Cunningham talk with Richie, and all is good with the world (*Happy Days* reference for you younger folks). Then they go off to college or get a job, move out, get married, have a couple of kids and you get to be Grandma and Grandpa. Everyone makes enough money and is relatively healthy, does not need a therapist and has wonderful tools to handle the chaos of life.

Completely unrealistic! But it's what we all want. The movies and TV shows tell us the same things. We should be wealthy, beautiful, happy and productive. And we should all send out cards at the end of the year showing off our happy faces and coordinating outfits to announce to our friends how great our life is. I cannot even write that without cringing.

Worry, worry, worry. Unfortunately I have to face the fact that in my situation, worry is judgment: When I'm worried about my son, it's because I'm judging him as not normal. I'm judging him less than perfect. And I need to stop. None of us are normal and none of our kids are perfect. Me worrying about the future of my son is rooted in my fear that I will not be able to emotionally handle his failures or where his illness might lead him. Recognizing worry is never productive can help make the connection that worry is really a fear of the uncontrollable future. Trust in yourself that you will be okay regardless of the outcome. You will notice that even genuine concern for another's safety or health can be filled with love rather than fear. Sending love to someone you are concerned about is always helpful. Worrying about them causes you to suffer and sends the message to the other person that you do not believe they are capable of handling their situation.

## Can We Stop Judging?

What if I stopped all worry about my child that is based in judgment? What if instead I loved them for all that they are? What if I simply stopped judging my child? And given children are mirrors into our own souls, what if I stopped judging everything?

That driver is an idiot for not hitting the gas at a green light.

My mother is so critical of me.

My child does not care that she is always late for school.

My brother is insensitive and a jerk. All he does is brag about how great his kids are when he knows how disabled mine are.
My wife is such a bitch sometimes.
My coworker is so lazy, always riding on the tails of my hard work.
My house is not clean enough.
I need to lose weight.
I am not attractive enough.
I should work harder.
I should have finished my degree.
I need to make more money.
I am embarrassed my child is overweight.
I wish my son was better at sports.
My kid is so smart.
My daughter is so pretty.
I love to brag about my grandchildren.

What if…
We are all equal because we are all one?

Step out of judgment, and teach your children to do the same. It's impossible to know what another person is like or what they are thinking, no matter how well you think you know them. I challenge kids and adults to come up with three reasons why someone behaved a certain way. It's fun because they quickly come up with far more than three possibilities, and they become curious instead of angry or judgmental.

Consider the possible reasons someone might cut you off in traffic. I once had a client who was completely convinced that anyone who cut her off in traffic was attacking her personally, and she would follow the other driver in a rage. I sometimes wonder if she's still alive because she absolutely refused to consider another way of looking at it. She was completely focused on herself, and all that resulted was that she was miserable and put herself in great peril.

So let's do this exercise. What are some examples of why someone might cut you off in traffic?

The person is spacing out.

The person just got some bad news and is distracted.

The person is an undercover cop trying to get somewhere quickly.

The person is in labor and needs to get to a hospital.

The person is angry and not acting like their true self.

The person is having a seizure (my favorite explanation because I am epileptic).

The person just learned how to drive (if you have ever driven with your 16-year-old, you really get this one).

The person is drunk.

The person is blind in their right eye.

The person really did not see me.

The person is rushing to the hospital to see their father before he passes away.

I could go on forever with examples, and notice, none of them have anything to do with "me."

You can use this strategy to consider why your child did not get invited to a party, why their teacher seemed angry, why their friend was mean to them, or why anyone did or said just about anything. I cannot tell you how many clients I have who are convinced they know their boss or co-worker or relative hates them. They share all of the "evidence" they have painfully collected over years. They say things like, "My boss walked right by me in the hall yesterday and did not even say hi. That bastard. He/she cannot even acknowledge me." No one likes it when I ask him or her if they acknowledged their boss.

I'll say, "Give me three reasons—other than your boss hates you—why he/she did not say hi in the hall?"

We go through as much evidence as it takes for the client to realize their story might not be 100% accurate. The story now has a crack in it. They start to become open to the notion they themselves are contributing to the relationship. One time I asked the client, "Did you say hi to your boss in the hall?" And the client answered, "No, because I knew the ass wouldn't say hi to me."

Now I challenge them to be the change they want to see in their boss. I tell them next time they pass their boss, do not wait—give their boss a warm and cheery, "Hello! Good morning!" with a huge smile. Keep doing that and see what happens. It's a miracle! Unless your boss is a sociopath (which is rare), they will respond. They cannot help but respond. It's human nature, and smiles and good moods are contagious.

## Replacing Judgment with Love

My little Jackie hands out hugs to anyone and everyone who doesn't run from her. She lights up rooms with her enthusiasm and love. She will talk to anyone and wants to know everything about that person. It's crazy but amazing at the same time. I've learned a lot from Jackie.

I was sitting in the bleachers of my old high school watching my nephew play football. I was noticing familiar people, not wanting to talk to them given my social anxiety. Leave it to my fearless five-year-old to say, "Hey, mom! This nice man over here, his son's number is 88, and his name is Matt, and he said he went to high school with you!" I was forced into a nice exchange with a man I went to school with for many years.

Jackie is socially fearless. She loves people. She showers the disabled children in her special classroom with so much love and affection it blows me away. It matters not to her whether they can express love in return. She is the energizer bunny of loving people no matter what is going on with them.

What would the world be like if we all had the capacity for love Jackie has? I've seen children who do not appear to be capable of expressing their emotions hug Jackie or allow her to be close to them in ways they do not allow others. They trust her because she wants nothing from them. She just loves them.

That's how we want our children to feel. Safe. We want them to know that we want nothing from them. We just love them. I always believed my parents would not love me if I messed up in some way, or did not live up to their standards—probably because they told me not to come home if I ever got arrested. They gave me a list of unforgivable acts. I took that as a broader message, "If you screw up, we will not be here for you."

Funny thing is, I've messed up a lot, and I often fail to live up to others' standards because I'm human. For a long time I lived in shame, believing I was unlovable. I loathed myself. It mattered not what my parents thought of me—I already hated myself. It was confusing because I felt like I was loving others. However, I was lonely because I did not allow others' love in, out of shame and feeling worthless.

Guess what happens when you reject someone's love? They typically sense it and move on. Many lonely people, including children, don't understand that they are lonely because they are not open to love. If you are lonely, find a way to shed the shame and unworthiness and start loving yourself, because this will open you up to the love of others and you will attract other humans like flies to honey. I had to work with therapists and spiritual teachers for years to find my way back to loving myself.

In addition to loving ourselves, it helps to remember we're all connected. What I do affects you. What you think affects me. If we were to embrace our oneness, we would stop judging. We would have compassion, empathy, and love for each other. We would honor and love our differences and diversity.

Have the compassion, patience, love and understanding for your children that you needed as a child, even if you never received it. "Do unto others as you would have them do unto you," will save you as a parent.

I don't know about you, but I do not want to be judged by anyone. It felt awful to be judged when I went through a divorce by the very people I believed with all my heart would have loved and supported me when I needed it the most.

Others judging me is all about them and their internal struggle. I was triggering painful emotions in them and to ease their own suffering, they cast judgment upon me. Which, in the end, caused me pain, because I am human and not Zen enough yet to not let it affect me. Their judgment did nothing to resolve their core issues other than to repress them. They will get to deal with their issues again and again (with or without me) until they heal. Yuck!

So why are we so judgmental of our children? That is one loaded question. You could spend thousands on therapy and not even scratch the surface of that beast! (Although, I highly recommend beginning to peel that onion ASAP, and a talented therapist is a great choice.)

Just as you do not wish to be judged (nothing pisses me off more than when people feel sorry for me because I have dyslexia), your kids are not served by your judgment.

Want to stop judging? Start anywhere. I stopped looking for wrinkles in my face every time I looked in the mirror and instead noticed features I found pretty. Stop cussing other drivers. Stop worrying about whether your outfit measures up to others and smile because that is what people tend to notice. Stop wishing for more money and be grateful for the abundance that exists in your life. Look at your child every morning and see the perfections that are already there: a perfect soul on their journey to learn about love and connection, no different than yourself. Offer them love, kindness, compassion and forgiveness. They are on their own journey, which should never be compared to the normal journey.

When you judge less you will be liberated. Your children will feel loved and safe. You will stand in wisdom more often and forgive yourself more quickly. You will experience freedom. This is the freedom Dr. Martin Luther King, Jr. preached. Freedom from judgment.

Guide them, love them, set firm boundaries, teach them, be the example for them—and never, never judge them.

Never judge yourself.

It's the answer to almost everything.

## Speaking Out

Many a mom I work with tell me their daughter is so sensitive that when she hears other kids gossiping about other girls, she feels awful inside. However, she wants to be friends with these other girls because, well, we all want to fit in socially. She is conflicted. She knows backstabbing and bashing others is wrong, yet she wants social acceptance.

Some girls become disgusted with themselves, wishing they could speak up for what is right, and not wanting social acceptance from such flawed humans. This applies equally to boys. Boys can be brutal with gossip and can aggressively try to cut down even their closest friends in an effort to make themselves feel better.

We've all been there. Think about the last time you were stuck in a conversation when someone made a racist statement that caused your toes to curl. Did you speak up in disagreement? Did you walk away? Did you declare racism to be a moral wrong? How did you feel about yourself later that day?

I tend to say all the things I would have wanted to say to these people to my husband later that day. He always asks me if I actually said those things to the person, and I shamefully say no. Then I start to judge the person who made the racist comment, justified by my self-righteousness, and I start to feel better. We judge others to feel better about ourselves.

At that moment, I am no better than the person who made the racist statement. I am judging another person. I have no right. I certainly would not want that person to judge me. I relentlessly judge myself without help from anyone else.

If we cannot find the courage to speak our truth directly to the person making a karmic no-no, we cannot turn around and judge them for their mistake.

Some people are open to hearing your point of view, and others are not. If you think you can trust the person who made the racist comment, you might take them aside in a quiet moment and let them know it was not okay with you. But people have to be relatively enlightened to be open to hearing this kind of feedback, and this is rare. Teenage girls most likely are not in the enlightened group. You might empathize with your daughter by saying how frustrating and confusing this situation is and that it happens to all of us.

Offer your daughter some comforting wisdom. It's not her job to save the souls of everyone who crosses her path. These other girls will learn their lessons eventually—our job is to manage ourselves. Your daughter, however, can be an example by not participating in the conversation and not saying cruel things herself. She can feel good about herself by being the change she wants to see in the world. She can seek to enlighten the world in healthy ways. Maybe there is a club dedicated to inclusion at her school. Maybe she could start one.

Most importantly, help her to avoid judgment of her friends. We can do this by honoring their struggle. They are imperfect humans seeking to find their way. We are also imperfect trying to find our way. We all make mistakes and hopefully learn from them. If we can empathize with another person's struggle, then we will stop judging, and we may even become curious as to why these girls are saying the things they are saying.

Are they hearing these things at home? Are they trying to fit in by saying these things? Do they really believe what is coming out of their mouths? Are they hurt because someone else judged them? I could come up with a million reasons why these girls deserve love and understanding instead of judgment. If we judge them, we are doing the very thing that we detest about them and their judgment.

But we cannot tell our children to stop judging others if we are doing it ourselves. It's a bitch isn't it? I have to model not judging the guy who flipped me off for not realizing the light turned green, not judging my boss who didn't give me a raise again this year, not judging my mother-in-law who never stops calling, not judging my neighbor whose dog craps on my lawn every morning, not judging the boyfriend from college who dumped me for my best friend, not judging the criminal who committed murder. See how hard this gets?

Wait! A murderer deserves to be judged, right? Well, we have a system of laws set up to impose consequences in such situations. I bet, though, if I told you the story behind why the murder occurred, you might be more empathetic. (I am not condoning murder. Do not write to me saying murder is wrong under all circumstances. I agree. Just listen.)

The young man who committed the murder killed his father who was beating his mother daily and raping his younger sister. The father was an alcoholic who beat him regularly. The young man did everything possible to protect his mother and sister, but could not be there around the clock because the father did not work so the son had to hold down two jobs to provide shelter and food for the family. He never was able to finish high school because he had to work. They lived in extreme poverty and had no way to leave their geographic location.

They tried to kick the father out with the help of some neighbors, but he always returned in a rage. The young man, after finding his mother barely alive from a beating and his sister sobbing over her, lost his temper and shot his father in a fit of rage. He is now a murderer serving a life sentence.

How do you feel now?

We do not know everyone's story. We do not know why they are behaving the way they are. We do not know their motivation or their history. We have not walked in their shoes. Who are we to judge? We do not know what other people are thinking, ever. So be curious. Be open. Do not judge.

CHAPTER 2

# *Gratitude*

I often find myself struggling with feeling sorry for myself. I forget the saying, "Be grateful for what you have." Gratitude can be found everyday and in every moment, however, gratitude is easy to miss.

Feeling sorry for oneself is emotional torture. I open Facebook and see what my old friends are doing and inevitably there is a picture of one of their children holding up a trophy for winning a baseball game or gymnastics meet, playing an instrument at a recital, or starting their own business. Their children are normal, even extraordinary. Holiday cards can also cause me to sigh and wonder what news I would want to share with acquaintances about my challenging family life.

News... what would my news be? If I had great news of even normal accomplishments they might include Joey learning to tie his shoes when he was fourteen so he could go bowling in his summer school PE class (he has since forgotten how to tie his shoes). Joey did learn to ride a bike at sixteen. Oh, how about the day we discovered mood-stabilizing medication! Or, the day Tommy exhibited deep remorse for setting the yard on fire. Maybe when Jackie learned her colors after years of prompting. No detentions for skipping PE? Finding a great neuropsychiatrist. The long awaited untreatable genetic syndrome diagnosis (that was actually a good day to finally have an answer). The sad part is I know there are parents out there who would kill for my seemingly trivial moments.

I can feel pretty down, even victimized, that our family victories do not measure up. Through this filter, the grass is always greener on the other side.

Then, there are those sobering moments in life that burn an image into my brain that keep me humble and remind me to be grateful for what I do have.

I was sitting at Chili's, the restaurant, with my youngest daughter and stepson, exhausted by life, praying to get through the meal without some scene erupting. I noticed a couple across the restaurant sitting quietly with their adult son who had to be strapped to his wheelchair. He could not speak or feed himself. He drooled. He made loud grunts. I watched them. My heart began to ache. Tears ran down my face uncontrollably. The couple was so quiet, so composed. The young man rocked against the constraining straps that kept him from falling out of his wheelchair.

Despite the loud noises their son made, they never flinched. They just kept their heads down and ate. They look tired. Not like "I haven't slept in a month tired," the kind of tired you experience from years of worry, fear and anger. Years of wondering:

"Can we endure this?"
"We did not choose this."
"I feel guilty for wishing for my child was normal."
"I cannot take anymore."
"I am so tired."
"Is my child happy?"
"What is the point of all of this?"

They will never be grandparents. They will never live apart from this child. They will never cheer for their son's victory in any sport. All they can hope for is the money not to run out, their relationship to endure one of life's most difficult challenges, and there to be someone to care for their son if, God forbid, he outlives them.

These people are my heroes. I look at this family, and I am humbled by their grace.

I am grateful for what I have.

CHAPTER 3

# *Ego*

Such a little word. Such a huge problem.

We've discussed judgment and gratitude. Now we need to dig into the abyss we call ego. Ego is often the driver of judgment and why we find it difficult to maintain a state of gratitude. It is our emotional self, which tends not to be the mature one. If you are curious as to why we all judge and how we might stop, it's necessary to understand ego.

Consider a two-year-old. We do not expect them to manage their emotions very well. Their mental capacities are not developed sufficiently enough so they can calm themselves. We accept the terrible twos as a part of life.

As we progress through our lifetime, we, hopefully, learn to soothe ourselves, or in other words, we learn how to manage our own ego. This is one of the main goals of growing and evolving as a human. We become wiser than our ego. Simply, I do not need to have a tantrum when I cannot have a cookie before dinner. I can calm myself by utilizing my amazing cortex to tell my inner child that it would be best to have the cookie after dinner so I can optimize my nutritional intake.

If someone had told me I could manage my ego with my brain when I was young, I might have been more successful along the way.

Call your ego anything you want: your inner child, the brat inside your brain who wants what it wants, your desire. If your ego is running the show, you might (raised eyebrow implying sarcasm, pause for dramatic effect)... be struggling.

Teenagers are wonderful examples of the ego creating chaos in life. They have very strong emotions and desires that can lead to impulsive decision-making.

The teenager has a thought and out it goes on the wings of a text message—no pause—no time to consider.

When I was a kid (damn - I never thought I would say that), we had to wait until we saw someone in person or until the phone was free (yes, the entire household shared one lousy phone which was stuck to a wall). It was the nightmare like it sounds. My entire sorority in college had two phones, which were in closets, and we made the pledges act as answering machines delivering little pieces of paper to the appropriate people. It was, truly, the dark ages. What my grandparents did, I haven't a clue. No selfies, no sexting, no constant contact.

Imagine all that personal space and quiet time. If grandma or grandpa wrote a nasty letter, they probably reread it because they were taught to proof their work, and then threw it away and never mailed it. Why? Because they had time to consider. What a beautiful thing... time to consider. Do I really want to say this? Maybe I'm just angry and now that I've written it all down, I realize that I am no longer as angry. They had time to cool off before letting the irretrievable text fly at the speed of light.

Grandma and Grandpa probably had a lot less drama because they worked out their internal angst before they mailed the letter, made the phone call or had a chance to talk to the person "in person." On the other hand, maybe today's ease of communication, in which we get to see people's unfiltered ego, is a blessing. It's a valuable thing to understand who someone really is. A 3:00 AM text asking if you still love them is a dead giveaway you have someone who is not okay on their own. Their ego is needy and is driving their behavior (or as I like to say, their inner child is driving the bus).

Humans are pretty interesting in that they can manage their emotions via their cortex. If we could not, we might behave more like animals, destroying whatever we feared, taking whatever we wanted, doing whatever pleased us in a particular moment. But we do not (at least not always); we consider the impact on others, the consequences to us and long-term impacts to our lives. We, as humans, have learned that it is in our best interest to consider others, because we need them for our survival.

Parents often struggle and are conflicted because they want to fulfill the desires and egoic wants of their children, whether it's their two-year-old wanting candy or a teenager wanting a $200 pair of shoes. We as parents do not want to experience the child who isn't getting what they want and cannot manage their emotions. It's unpleasant. Teenagers are the masters of manipulating their parents to get what they want. After enough whining and begging and complaining, the parent can't stand it anymore, and they give the kid just about anything to get them to go away. It works beautifully. We parents—I have been one in many moments—are fooled into believing these "needs" a child has are real. But they are not; they're simply the ego run amuck. I'm thinking that if I give the kid the candy or the $200 shoes, they will stop. But they don't stop. They soon come back for another round, with another "need"... like a gambler hoping to hit the jackpot again.

We need to meet the actual needs of the child, not their unmitigated desire. Desire is insatiable. It never stops. Desire is not supposed to stop, because at some point in our evolutionary history, it kept us alive and reproducing. Now, it feeds our economy. The child does not know that the objects of her desire will not satisfy her. A wise adult knows this. They can overcome their ego and consider whether the object they desire is truly necessary and within their means to acquire.

We fear what might happen if we do not meet the desires of our children. Maybe my child will not love me anymore. Maybe other people might judge me as a bad parent. Maybe I will feel like a failure because my self-worth is tied up in presenting a happy, attractive, productive child (at its core this is shame and guilt).

A wise, loving parent sees past the tantrum the child's ego is throwing and looks to the actual need of the child—the need to learn how to manage one's own ego and desire, the need to learn self-control. The wise parent models this and provides loving boundaries for a child by not caving to the desire of the child. It can be tricky to do this without triggering your own shame or guilt if you have an addiction to giving in to your own momentary desires, such as buying whatever you want in the moment (whether you can afford it or not). If this is your issue, stop and think about how long that desire stays satisfied. Get help so you are not modeling this to your kids even while you may be saying something completely different to them.

All of this is easier said than done, and I'm terrible at setting boundaries. I'm constantly looking for ways to set some kind of boundary while also allowing my kids to get what they want. It's pretty ugly. I set firm consequences for toxic behavior and after a couple of days, hours, or even seconds, I start to soften. For example, I take away the cell phone for a week because my daughter has missed the bus yet again even though I lay out her clothes and bring her breakfast in bed and pack her lunch and her backpack. (All she has to do is get out of bed, put on her clothes and get in the car for the eighth-mile ride down the hill.) Her whining and cajoling begins. I start to feel uncomfortable and I say, "You can earn back your phone if you get out of bed the first time I tell you to for the next three days." What am I thinking?

Despite our challenges (mental, emotional or physical), we can evolve and mature our ego. The more the adult in the room matures their ego and models self control, the better chance the child can emulate the parent. If the parent has uncontrolled desire that oozes out in inappropriate ways, the child will model that. Often we judge our kids for their unrealistic demands, when we ourselves may not have learned to manage our own desire for new cars, bigger homes, extravagant vacations and designer clothing. Desire can be materialistic (e.g. clothes, cars, houses, stuff that plugs in) or emotional (e.g. needing validation from others to feel good about ourselves) or mental (e.g. never ending schooling, reading) or physical (e.g. exercise, sex).

You might be wondering how, exactly, to help your ego mature. Step one is recognizing you have an inner child. The next step is to give that inner child a real voice, and listen to what it says. Then allow your wise self to parent and care for the child (be gentle with yourself). Once that inner child starts to trust you and feel your love, it will mature. Your sense of control over your world will increase. You will feel more calm, clear and satisfied. You will start driving the bus instead of your ego being in the driver's seat. This process mirrors the way we would want to handle a real child. We would want to be loving, patient, trusting, and wise.

Maybe we did not get that feeling as a child ourselves. I do not know any person who does not have a story from childhood that is still causing some upheaval in their life. It's now time to give your inner child everything it needs, such as unconditional love and acceptance. If you can do this for yourself (or with the help of a great counselor), you'll rock as a parent.

You will be the change you want to see in the world (and in your children). Thanks, Gandhi...again.

Here's another way to make sure your ego doesn't get in the way of parenting your kids. Acknowledge that what's important to you (and your ego) may not be important to your child. You are different people, after all. Do you need them to have a clean room, get straight A's, and to be on time? Or is it something you desire? Instead of imposing your desire upon them (and if you are dealing with a teenager, this is always a losing battle), stop. Recognize this is something you want, not something you need. That alone can calm your emotional turmoil. Then ask yourself how you might help your child see the importance of a clean room or good grades—without getting your ego or self-worth involved. Another option would be to let go of the need for a perfectly tidy room (as long as it's not a health hazard) and honor that not everyone "needs" everything to be tidy.

When you're watching your child battle with their ego when they're not getting their way, tell them, "I see how difficult this is for you right now."

Teach them breathing techniques to calm themselves. Teach them they can talk to themselves to help soothe their emotions. Teach them that emotions are not permanent states (thank you, Dr. Dan Siegel). Teach them that time is a gift that allows us to consider and come back to a state of love. Honor their battles as you should honor your own egoic struggles. It is hard to be patient with one's own ego and that of our children. We must be gentle. You know you learned best from those loving, patient teachers (maybe you had one or two during your education). Why wouldn't you want to be that for yourself and your children?

The battle to manage one's own desire and raw emotion is at the core of every war, drama and argument that has ever existed. It is time we brought this out into the light instead of judging others. We judge others because we either do not like what we are seeing in ourselves, or we do not like what others expose about us.

Many moms condemn other moms for "doing too much for their children." Moms that have to take their kids to multiple specialists

(OT, PT, psychologists, vision therapy, tutors, psychiatrists, doctors, etc.) get handed this judgment a lot. They should get loving support; instead they often get slapped with the hand of judgment (especially from grandmothers). My own ex-mother-in-law actually said to me, "No wonder he is so anxious, all he does is go to the doctor."

These moms hear over and over, "Just leave the poor kid alone. They'll be fine. Look at my kid. He's just fine." What are these people really saying?

Here's what they're saying: "What you're doing to help your child makes me feel guilty because I do not believe I do enough for my children." Or, "I'm ashamed because I believe no one loved me enough to exhibit the same amount of love and care for me."

When someone judges, it is all about him or her. Stop taking everything so personal (thank you, Kimberly).

Next time your teenager is trying to guilt you into something (e.g. letting them attend a co-ed sleepover) that you know is not in their best interest, look them in the eye, see their wise, grounded, capable self, and with every ounce of love in every cell in your body, say "No."

Remember you do not need to give a reason. There is never a need to defend love. Then, be prepared to remind them of all the tools they have at their disposal to manage their own disappointment. Give yourself a hug, and know you met their need, not their desire. They got an opportunity to practice managing their internal brat who sometimes leaks out. I am stressing the word practice because they may not have been very successful and may need to try again a few thousand times.

All is good, even if they are in an emotional rant. You can choose to be affected or not. Really.

CHAPTER 4

# "Where are My Fucking Cheez-its?"

Now, this story needs to be told if for no other reason than it is hilarious. It also relates to egoic struggles.

At one point in my life I had all four of my children enrolled at the same private school for gifted children. I was privileged to serve this wonderful little school as a member of the Board of Trustees, an odd job if I do say so. A school board member of any kind has one of the most thankless jobs on the planet. No pay, no benefits, meetings in the evening, meetings during the summer, legal nightmares, entitled parents who call at all hours of the night, crazy parents who will yell at you about their child's math curriculum (which board members have nothing to do with), and teachers who give you the eye every time they pass you in the hall. So, if you volunteer as a board member of any non-for-profit, I tip my hat to you. Anyway, I was a board member for the school. I took this role very seriously and one of my jobs was to be an exemplary parent (whatever that really is). The problem was my children were not exactly exemplary children.

So, one day I was chatting with a group of women in the parking lot discussing who knows what about the school. The conversation was somewhat serious as any conversation amongst moms about school can be. I was trying to be a professional, listening and taking in as much as I could without blurting my real opinion, when my precious little preschooler, Jackie, walked up to me and shouted, "Where are my fucking Cheez-its?!?"

I thought my friend Kathy was going to die of laughter, while I dropped my head in embarrassment and defeat. Jackie was this super tiny, super cute, super sweet, little muffin of a four-year-old. She wore a faux cheetah jacket and a rust colored hat with a giant flower on the front of it. So, hearing her swear like a trucker and demand her "fucking Cheez-its" was seriously hilarious in the moment. However, my image was completely blown. My ego was crushed. I could say nothing.

Now, Jackie swore all of the time, although she usually saved it for her home or siblings. I could show you her neuropsychological evaluations and brain scans to help you understand the why behind Jackie's sensory seeking behavior (and dropping f-bombs gets lots of attention when you are 4), however, the story behind Jackie would derail the point of how I responded as a parent.

Why was I so embarrassed? I felt like a failure as a parent in front of people from whom I was so desperately seeking approval. My role as a board member allowed me to feel important again, like I once did when I worked and got paid. While I did not get paid, the job came with a certain amount of respect and prestige (even though in reality the job is not as glamorous and powerful as most people believe). At this point in my life I was still seeking validation through the approval of others, which, by the way, is not a good strategy if you haven't already figured that out. If you are trying to impress others by being the perfect parent, let me fill you in on a little secret. No one really thinks about you that much. Minus a few enlightened ones, most humans focus mainly on themselves. So, if we worry about what others think of us, we can comfort ourselves a bit knowing that most people are not thinking about us at all. And if they are thinking about us, it is typically run through their own judgmental filters, so they can feel better about themselves.

I am getting ahead of myself here. My point is around entitlement and shame. Little Jackie felt entitled. She felt entitled enough to unleash the f-bomb on me in front the very people I was trying to impress with my sophistication. I have learned that little Jackie is one of life's greatest teachers, hands down, ever. She is completely unfiltered. You cannot hide from her or her issues. She basically grabbed my unhealthy, shame-filled desire for external validation and threw it in my face. I felt naked, exposed. She was completely fine. And, yes, she got her Cheez-its in the car. I asked her to try to refrain from using the f-word (even though I knew, given her issues, it was futile) and asked her to make a nice request such as, "May I please have some Cheez-its?"

So, while Jackie was acting entitled, I always remember that moment and wonder if she is not much wiser than the rest of us. (She's sometimes scary that way.) I have reframed the incident to be a reminder to me that Jackie felt entitled to expose my shame. In my head, I could almost hear her thoughts, "Who are you kidding, Mom? No one is buying this crap."

The wisdom here is that the only person I need to seek approval from is myself. I have lived at least forty years hoping to be validated by other people. Guess what? No one showed up to validate me in the way I wanted. It took me a long time to learn that my opinion of myself is the most important. No one can possibly understand all that I deal with in a day. No one could ever begin to recognize the sacrifice I have made on behalf of my children. No one notices how hard I work.

So, when I finally realized that the only person who could know everything about my sacrifices, my emotional angst, my exhaustion, my unending effort, was me, I found freedom. I pat myself on the back regularly. Every moment that I make a decision that is in line with my values and my heart, I feel joy. There is no resentment. How can I resent myself? When I was waiting for my children's father to validate me, he fell short of my very high expectations. I did not complain. Instead, I grew a giant knot of resentment over fifteen years. I know now that resentment is the death of relationships. So, with my husband, I work diligently to expose those moments when I start to feel resentment towards him. Together we look for the underlying story or belief (which for me is typically, and rather boringly, shame that I am unlovable or unworthy) that is causing me to feel resentful. He lovingly listens and has faith in me to deal with it. He owns his part if he believes that to be necessary. It works. Try it.

And just so you know, Jackie who is now 11, continues on her quest to uncover everyone's façade on a daily basis. We have not gotten her to stop dropping f-bombs. I think she might be an alien.

CHAPTER 5

# Everything is Not Okay

That moment with Jackie was hard. Being a parent is hard.

In Chicago, the winters can be brutally cold. Things that are frozen tend not to smell. Then in the spring thaw, those frozen smells birth a new life, some lovely and some absolutely noxious.

I was getting out of the minivan the other morning after driving my eighth grader to the bus stop (yes, really, an eighth of a mile downhill). I noticed a familiar smell. Not a good smell yet it evoked some pleasant memories of strolling through the zoo when the kids were younger. You know when you are happily strolling by elephants, zebras, and camels, there is that little voice in the back of your mind that says, "Damn! That smells freaking awful!" (Don't get me started on the penguin house. Why isn't anyone gagging from that smell?) But you are at the zoo and that is supposed to be an iconic, warm family moment. Like those families that homeschool their kids with ease, eat organic, swear their kids have never been through a McDonald's drive-through, and do not watch TV. You long to be the family that finds time to go to the stinking zoo twice a month and signs up for educational tours and actually reads the signs in front of the cages.

Any other place on Earth (I am thinking the subway in Paris on a hot day or Chinatown in Manhattan in the summer) you would cover your mouth and immediately search for an escape. Not at the zoo. We walk slowly, smiling, pretending the smell is not there, and we are enjoying life.

My point here, other than to reveal that my minivan smells like a damn zoo, is that in life, especially around our kids, we pretend (because we think we should be enjoying ourselves) like everything is okay. People ask us, "How are the kids?" You feel the bile rise from the pit of your stomach, smile and say, "Fine, great."

I love being a Mom. Best job on the planet!

Really?

Let's be honest, this job by any evaluative standard would come out at the bottom of any list. No pay, no boss offering you feedback of any kind, no benefits, no breaks (this is a reality for many parents either physically or emotionally or both), and no vacation. You cannot convince me dragging your kids through Disney World is a vacation. Every other kid is crying from complete sensory overload. I am never more exhausted than I am after a "family" vacation. (I love Disney World when I go without my kids.)

I do not pretend to know the answer to the dilemma that the job of parenting blows (sorry if you were expecting some comfort here). However, I'm curious about parents who never expose their children to fast food, TV, video games, or cell phones. Are they wise or are they sending their children into the world unprepared? We often talk to our kids about how to manage their decisions about drugs, alcohol, peer pressure and even sex. But do we really teach them to manage their relationship with fast food? My point is there are so many ways that addictions can manifest, it is important to help your child learn moderation on all fronts. These choices will become a daily challenge, especially after they get a driver's license. The beacon of the golden arches is still a demon I must face daily. My 16-year-old has recently discovered how much food he can buy at Taco Bell for very little money.

So, let's be real with our children. Zoos smell bad. Being a parent is hard, and we deserve breaks. And, the real world is full of addictive things and helping your child learn how to choose what is best for them is the most important thing. You can shield and protect all you want, but someday soon, they are going to be out there. You will be nowhere to be found, and they will need to choose. So, if you decide to never have fast food (more power to ya!), explain to your children why you are making that choice so when they go off to college or their own apartment, they do not become a junkie because it was the forbidden fruit throughout their childhood.

And as for parenting being hard, own it. It is a hard job. No one is going to give you an award. However, you can pat yourself on the back everyday knowing you did the best you could given your resources. We do not hug ourselves enough or tell ourselves we're great. Our brains are not sophisticated enough to really distinguish between me telling me or someone else telling me. So, if you are needing some validation, give it to yourself, and see how you feel after a month of doing it everyday. And if you go to bed knowing you did not do your best, keep reading and give yourself a hug anyway. You need one.

CHAPTER 6

# Why Do We Stop the Kids from Fighting?

You know what else is really hard about parenting? Watching your kids fight with each other.

You know how you get angry at refs for not letting teams "just play," or allowing boxers to just fight? Why is that? It's because you know the interference doesn't allow the appropriate outcome of the game or match to manifest. How many NCAA Final Four basketball games have you watched that were impacted by a bad call? What if we, as parents, are interfering with our children's lives in that very same manner?

I picture God looking down on our regular episodes of Tommy making annoying sounds for 57 minutes triggering Joey to finally crack and go after him. All hell breaks loose, and the main event begins. Just when the fight really gets good, I (the ref) step in and rip them apart. I can feel God patiently saying, "Never fear, I can book a rematch tomorrow." This loop goes on and on.

What are we doing in those moments when we step between our daughters who each literally have a fist full of hair? While I am not suggesting allowing major bloodshed, I ponder what would happen if we allowed our children to solve their own problems. They might actually come to their own resolutions.

That is a necessary life lesson: how to work out your problems with another person. I think that's why siblings were invented.

CHAPTER 7

# The Manual

You are not given a manual when your child is born. Given how hard it is to be a parent, you'd think they would pop out of the womb with one tied to their foot or something. How to get my kids to stop fighting and bickering with each other might be the first chapter I would flip to if there were such a manual.

There are lots of books out there, but there's precious little actual help. Unfortunately if something goes wrong or your child is "out of the box," to put it lightly, you're screwed. One would imagine that when a family member gives birth to a child with special needs, the family would rally around the parents to support them. They would learn as much as possible to support them. They would offer to take the child to countless doctor and therapist appointments. This has not been my observation. Let's say your child has autism. You may have observed your family, in moments, scatter like roaches in a spot light.

Most people cannot handle the emotional and physical burden of coping with a disabled child. I know there are probably wonderful families who rally together to support a parent who just learned their child is deaf or has AD/HD. If you are a member of one of those families—count your lucky stars. I have yet to witness one in all my years. I talk with the parents I work with or meet in the waiting rooms of therapists' offices (OT, PT, vision, behavioral, social, whatever). I have heard their stories. These parents are alone, misunderstood, blamed, ostracized, exhausted, and abandoned by those who "should" be there for them.

I remember one mom who spent her entire day, everyday, trying to help her developmentally delayed and sometimes violent son. Endless therapies, special schools, constant worry about how to get through the day, the school year, and God help her, the rest of her life. The little brother, about four years old, lived in fear of his brother's emotional outbursts. His brother had physically hurt him. The mom was giving everything she had and more to manage a seemingly impossible situation. She told me her family had abandoned her, and her husband hid at work pretending there was nothing wrong. She had no time to think of herself. She was war-torn, literally. All I could offer her was compassion and an open heart, silently listening.

Please, do not turn your back to these parents. If you are one, find help. Pay for a therapist to listen to you. Ask your friends and family for help. You may need to shout it from the mountaintops. You cannot and should not have to do this alone. And when no one responds, know this: when you help yourself, you help those around you. If you want to help your kids, help yourself. The greatest growth and maturity I have ever seen in my children is when I have done my own work on my own issues and have cared for myself.

I wish that every parent could have a coach, someone in their corner helping them to find their way through the maze of parenthood. If you don't have that, then take your self-care into your own hands. Use a fresh towel when you shower. Shower everyday (I have trouble finding time for this one). Do not allow your dinner to be the leftovers from the kid's meals. Find someone who will help you get a break.

Churches can be wonderful places to find experienced adults who care and would be willing to help. Think outside the box. We have hired college kids on break or looking for jobs and empty nest neighbors who are thrilled to be needed again. You are important not only to your children but also to yourself. You deserve more.

When I was in the midst of my divorce and in a state of complete shock, panic, and fear, I went to a spa in another state for 4 days. Something I would have never, ever considered previously. My oldest son, Joey, the boy I worry about day and night, said to me when I returned, "Oh, good! I don't have to worry about you anymore. You know that house across the street that they are building? You know it did not look all that stable without the walls in place. Now that the bricks are up, the house feels solid. That's how you feel to me now, Mom. You feel more solid."

I was blown away. I stood there with my mouth agape. This 13-year-old boy who I worried about from the moment he was born, was experiencing anxiety because he sensed my anxiety. Our children love us. They want us to be okay. Everyone knows smiles are contagious. Well, so are fear, anxiety, guilt and shame. I do not care how well you think you are hiding it. Our children sense our emotions. This is common knowledge about babies. Babies can sense when a young mother is anxious or not confident. Well, sorry to tell you, this sensing never ends.

If you do not take care of yourself for you, do it for your child. I personally want my girls to learn that being a mom does not mean giving oneself away. I am important. I deserve to be loved and respected (especially by me).

CHAPTER 8

# *Reflections*

Let's see if we can come up with something that resembles a manual. And, by the way, this manual applies to more than parenting.

Our kids are walking, talking mirrors of us. You know it to be true. You see how you mimic your own parents. I hear my mom's voice coming out of my mouth, and I am so frustrated. We pick up all kinds of idiosyncrasies from our family members. I noticed in a picture of my older brother and me sitting at a table in Mexico having lunch that we had the exact same posture, and we both held our hand in front of our mouth in the exact same way. It was creepy. We copy each other. We learn by watching how others cope and behave. I am not going to get into the neuroscience behind this—it's a hotbed of controversy. However, I think we all know that our environment has a huge part to play in who we become, especially the people in that environment.

This means the things that drive us crazy about our kids are really in us. And we hate that. Our kid is impulsive and makes stupid decisions. We hate that about them, and more to the point, we hate that we are impulsive and have made bad decisions. Our kid puts on a false persona in front of his friends, and you hate that. And, oh! We cannot be ourselves at work; we hate that about ourselves. Our college student is driving us nuts because they are so unhappy not doing what they are passionate about but what they think will make others happy. We tell them we just want them to be happy when, secretly, we are detesting our own job but see no way out because we have to pay the mortgage. See a pattern here?

Damn! That means "do as I say, not as I do" is neurologically ridiculous and impossible. They are mirroring us, no matter what we say. My parents told me, "do as I say, not as I do," almost daily. It rings in my ears like a Def Leppard concert. We absolutely take on our parents' issues. And unless we consciously become aware of it, we become our parents (or some messed up version of them).

My dad wanted/needed control of his world, so he yelled at everyone and everything to keep them in line (it doesn't work very well, in case you're considering it). I swore I would never yell at people, because I hated it so much when I was growing up. I swore I would never become my father around my kids. Well, I missed the proverbial boat here. While I do not yell like him (although I lose it occasionally—I'm human), I unintentionally grabbed on to the reason he was yelling and made it my own. He wanted to feel safe. I need control to feel safe. So when my kids do not perform as expected, when life feels out of control, when people are unpredictable (imagine that!), I do not yell because I swore I would never do that. However, I cling to my inherited belief that I must control things, or I will not be okay, and I become anxious, perfectionistic and ruthlessly judge myself as a failure. I internalize my anxiety, while my dad externalized it. And bingo! I have become my father. Ugh.

Once I became aware of my faulty belief, I could forgive myself (because I am human) and my dad (because he is human). I apologize to poor 'ole dad for being angry with him because he is unaware of his belief that is driving his behavior, and I replace my belief with my truth. For me, the truth is that I do not need to—and cannot—control anything but my own ego. I am completely fine amidst the chaos that is life.

CHAPTER 9

# *Could It Be You?*

Speaking of forgiving yourself, it's an amazing day when you wake up to the thought that you may be the one messing up your kid with your unconscious stories, beliefs and desires.

I realized I had an unconscious fear that I would not be okay without my oldest son being enmeshed with me. He was the first human to accept my love. It is incredible when someone actually receives your love. With so many of us struggling with shame issues, I wonder how many of us are really open to receiving love.

I do an exercise with groups that I learned in coach training where one person faces another and tells them all the wonderful things they see in that other person. I am always amazed at how uncomfortable the receiver looks. Many express a desire to run out of the room. Many—and this is why the receiver is not allowed to speak through the entire exercise—try to minimize the compliments afterwards with comments like, "If you really knew me…"

At the university where I learned about the healing arts, my classmates called me "Precious" as a nickname during one class. They viewed me as a gentle, kind and loving soul. Ha! If they only knew the real me. The truth is, they were seeing the real me. I was the one twisting reality to fit my own distorted, unkind perception of myself. We humans can be harder on ourselves than anyone else.

My fear that I would not be okay without Joey being completely dependent on me was messing with his head. He started to believe he needed to remain helpless so that I could be okay. What a disaster. If I know I am okay without him needing me, he'll sense it and end his need to be helpless in an effort to care for me.

I am, in part, the cause of my son's stunted development. Having learned this, I am now showing the world I am okay. I'm embracing the idea that I have more to do and give the world than being Joey's mom. My kids will notice I have stepped into my power, and they'll stop caretaking me, even if they are doing it subconsciously.

CHAPTER 10

# No, Really, the Umbilical Cord was Cut at Birth

Let's discuss what was going on with Joey and me, because we are not the only parent-child team doing this enmeshment thing.

There is a concept called energetic cording. You might be able to visualize a glowing rope made of energy connecting you to your child (or anyone, especially, cough, your own parents). Most parents understand this concept when I say, "You know that feeling, that surge of energy, when you watch your child almost (or actually) fall down the stairs?" Or, remember the pain you felt when your child did not get invited to a birthday party and all his friends did. If you are a typical human, you internally prepare yourself to go find that kid and punch him/her in the face. Remember watching your first baby climb on the bus for the first day of school and walking into the house feeling like something was missing? I have to admit by my fourth, I internally had the "Thank God!" response, but that's another chapter.

We can be very aware of our cording to our children. I believe this cording is necessary in the very beginning just as an umbilical cord is necessary, and as our children grow in independence, the cord should gradually lessen in strength until it is completely gone by the time they reach a certain age (which is probably different for every child).

We also can be unaware we are corded to someone. These are the cords that wreak havoc in our lives. We may not even want to be corded to these people. I have an example of this type of cording.

My father, although he may never admit it, was corded to his mother. My own mother tells, with a touch of resentment and a sprinkling of anger, the story of the required dinner at Grandma's house every Sunday. The dinners were weekly when my parents were younger according to legend, and as we kids grew older the dinners occurred a little less frequently. I'm not sure if my mom ever complained to my dad about having to drag the three of us out to Grandma's house, which was not nearby, for a dinner that was always a challenge to the senses.

I do not know how to say this more tactfully, given that I loved my grandma despite her poor mental health: The food smelled funky. I'm not exactly sure how long in advance she prepared some of the food, but one would have to guess at least a couple of days, based on the dehydrated look of the shrimps. The meat was almost to the jerky stage. The dishes were never completely clean. There was no dishwasher so the dishes were, well, sticky. And my favorite was the watered down ketchup. Ugh.

This is a tangent but it speaks to the difficulty we all had in consuming the food my grandmother so lovingly prepared. On a few occasions, I slept over at grandma's house. I loved parts of it. We walked to the dime store, and I could pick out one thing, whatever I wanted, no matter how junky it might have been. That was awesome! I got to sleep on the couch, which I thought was cool because my grandpa would stay up and watch the news and then "The Tonight Show" with Johnny Carson. I felt special and mature, almost cool for a 6-year-old. And then came breakfast.

The plastic cereal bowls had a smell that was indescribable. The milk was weird and the Cheerios stale. My grandfather would take half of a banana and slice it up and put it on the Cheerios, leaving the other half to turn black by the next day. Yes, I typically got the black banana on my cereal. My grandparents were children of the Great Depression, so they would drink the milk left in the cereal bowl. It was not enough that I had to choke down the cereal, which I was completely disgusted by; I had to drink the milk after. I am now lactose intolerant. I have never eaten cereal since, and I cannot be around anyone who does. As soon as my bananas show any sign of color other than green or yellow, I have to throw them away.

It was like an unspoken law when we were little that we had to go to Grandma's for dinner, even though no one enjoyed it, including my dad. Somehow my dad believed he would not be okay or his mom would not be okay (at this point, it doesn't matter who is not okay) if he didn't show up every Sunday for dinner. The odd part was that no one ever felt better after dinner. Grandma complained she did not see us enough and asked when she would see us again. She could never be present and enjoy what was right in front of her. My dad would meet demand after demand, and he still felt a never-ending guilt, which I believe stayed with him until the day Grandma passed.

Cording can create a positive feeling. For example, when your kid scores a goal or makes the cheerleading squad you jump out of your seat and scream as if they just won an Olympic gold medal. I remember dancing around my empty kitchen when I received my oldest son's acceptance letter to college along with an unexpected, hefty scholarship. I was giddy, elated, on top of the world! I called my son and his father, who at the time were in New York, to share the amazing news. I was flying high for the rest of the night. I was not thinking about the reality that there was no chance Joey was ready to go off to college. I reacted with more enthusiasm to this moment than almost any other moment in my own life. Why?

I was—and still am in moments—enmeshed or energetically corded to my son. When good things happen for him, I am ecstatic. When things are tough for him, I am depressed. He looks to me to answer a question, even at nineteen. I prompt him constantly and unconsciously. We are energetically corded to one another. When he is anxious, I am his go-to person. This is unhealthy for both of us. We need to be okay regardless of the condition of the other person.

Codependence looks awfully similar. I know many couples completely codependent on each other. It is really a wonderful feeling to know you are okay no matter what is going on in the lives of the people around you. I am not saying that you should not love and support your family and friends. There is a healthy way to do this. What I am saying is that your well-being should not become dependent on the well-being of another person. You can be empathetic and have your emotions. What you cannot do is use the other person as a compass for your own life. You need to guide yourself and make decisions that are in your own best interest. How many parents do you know who make decisions based on the needs of their children without even considering themselves for one second. This is not healthy for the parent or the child.

As for my grandma, she needed to be okay being alone. If that would have ever occurred for her, then she could have enjoyed our company when she had it instead of living in fear of not having it in the future. My dad needed to believe he was free to give of himself. Instead, he felt obligated. Obligated never feels good. The cord between my dad and his mom needed to be cut. Loving relationships are not made of obligations and expectations. Only when we give of ourselves freely can we feel whole.

Thus, I circle back into modeling the life you would want your child to lead along with making sure you are sane so you can be the best version of you, to be able to parent your children in the way you want.

In addition, when you are corded to someone else, you are putting some serious pressure on that other person. If you are corded to your child, not only do they have to be concerned about their own reactions and emotions and heartbreak, they now have the added pressure of your well-being. How many of us have been sick with worry or concern? Children sense that and mirror it right back at us.

What if we gave our love unconditionally? We did this when our babies learned to walk. We smiled and encouraged them no matter how many times they fell down. We cheered them for their effort and told them to try again with all the pride and love we could offer. When did we lose this mentality? When did we stop offering our children unconditional love? Do you smile at their failures and lovingly tell them to try again? Somewhere along the way, our well-being gets wrapped up in their well-being and failure becomes something we hate to feel.

Wouldn't it be incredible if we smiled with love at our children for their efforts and offered them unending patience? How else will they learn? How else will they know failure is literally our greatest learning opportunity?

Take care of yourself and know in your heart that you will be okay no matter what as long as you are offering unconditional love to your children and to yourself.

CHAPTER 11

# Being in Now

Grandma could not enjoy the moment of now. Can you? She was mentally ill—what's your excuse? I make up all kinds of excuses, but in reality, I need to stop and enjoy now.

We fear the future, and we judge the past. Meaning—I'm pissed about what happened, I judge it as bad, and I continually feel emotions about it. It is a fascinating form of self-torture.

The story we make up about an event is typically shaped by our perception of our childhood. Because of this childhood story (e.g. "I am unlovable because my parents did not meet my need"), we become vigilant about situations where we might be vulnerable to feeling this emotion again. We realize that humans are flawed and cannot be trusted (just like our parent(s)). We then develop a stronger story that we cannot trust anyone. People will always let us down eventually. (Well, duh, of course they will. They are human. None of us are perfect.)

Then we begin to collect data. We begin to notice all the moments when people are letting us down and are proving our story to be true. The ego likes to prove itself right. Our brain also likes to be right. We are stuck in a neural rut. We miss all the wonderful moments when people were there for us and offered their love and support. We're only focused on the negative. The world becomes a bleak place.

We also forget a universal truth in all of this. The only person you need to trust is you. This is self-reliance at its core. You and I are okay, and have no need for others to validate our existence or worthiness. I do not care if you are in prison or a priest—you are worthy of love and acceptance. You are human, and we are all here to learn and grow. Some of us have just chosen tougher lessons than others.

Ours is not to judge. Judgment breeds separation and self-loathing because at your deepest level you know you are just as flawed as the rest of us. If you are judging others you are guaranteed to be judging yourself, only probably more harshly. And that, my friend, will leave you feeling powerless. You will seek power in all the wrong places (work, school, relationships). You will never look inside and realize the power you seek is within you.

This is a form of externalizing your world. The result of this vicious merry-go-round is that you become a victim of uncontrollable events occurring all around you. It's like going to Vegas and saying, "If I roll a seven, I will be happy, and if I roll an eleven, I will be devastated."

This is not a powerful way to walk through life. You cannot control anything. You can try, but look at the weather. Who can stop a tornado or a hurricane or . . . having a child with Downs-Syndrome? All we can do is find our inner strength, love and wisdom and seek our path. We can choose suffering (yes, Buddha is correct, suffering is optional), or we can choose to take the high road. I can stand in my own power and follow my knowing—which sometimes means following my heart and not my head.

A worthy goal in life is to let go of judgment. I am not talking about evaluating a situation, which is wise. I am talking about judging something to be good or bad and basing your emotional state on it.

For me, it sounded like, "I don't know what is going to happen in the future, so I remain in a state of constant anxiety and fear of the future."

In all of this anxiety and judgment, we miss the beauty and the gift of now.

I was lying in bed fretting over the turmoil I continued to experience in my family, worrying that it would never get better. Would my husband's depression pass soon? Would Joey ever be okay? Would Tommy ever realize his toxic words are not healthy? Would Kelly ever start to care? Would Jackie's brain ever turn on? Blah, blah, blah…

What I suddenly realized was I was missing the very beautiful moment of now. I was sleeping in (a rarity). My little Jackie was curled up next to me with her arms wrapped around me. (She snores, but it's still cute.) My husband had a full night's sleep—something for which I had been praying. The house was quiet. In that moment, everything was perfect, wonderful. I had my family right there. Everyone was safe and relatively healthy. I felt loved and at peace as soon as I stopped worrying about the future and judging the past.

Try it!

CHAPTER 12

# *Urgency*

I even hate the word.

Urgency.

Just one more thing interfering with being in the now.

Everything feels so unbelievably urgent these days. Our poor kids have deadlines, homework, work, projects, social engagements, lessons, and sports. Not to mention the never-ending pressure to be beautiful, successful, wealthy…

And the faster this all happens, the better. We all know the smart kid finishes first, right? (Actually, I would argue to my grave that this is not true.). Only now are we beginning to recognize the value of the brain that processes slowly. These brains tend to process more and in new and different ways. But we value "fast," especially in the U.S. We are always timing everything. What is the point?

Time is a gift we can use to think before we act. Time was not given to us to fear or to use as some kind of tool to invoke guilt, shame or failure. Ask the slowest kid in school how he feels about himself. I have a hypermobility disorder, so I cannot run fast no matter how hard I try. I still feel the humiliation of coming in last, over and over. It's stupid when you think about it. What does running faster than another human have to do with my self worth? It makes sense if I'm outrunning a bear. Fortunately, my lack of speed has not cost me my life yet.

We still give trophies for first place—the fastest. We set unrealistic deadlines to complete projects in superhuman timeframes. We praise young people who rise to the top of their professions by the age of 24. We are always hurrying to be on time because we pack too many things into our schedule so that being "on time" requires superhuman effort. We drive ourselves nuts with this sense of urgency.

Not all cultures are like this. The Western culture is—and it's a major health crisis. Doctors will tell you about the unhealthy levels of cortisol and norepinephrine coursing through our brains everyday when stressed.

Now, I value my wise agreements with people and so should our children. If I say I am going to be somewhere at a certain time to meet someone, I should honor that agreement. It is disrespectful to the teachers or the other children or your co-workers to be late. It impacts others negatively. So the dilemma is how to be punctual without all the urgency. (Urgency is called for in the ER and at life threatening moments, not in getting to ballet lessons on time).

Look underneath that urgent feeling. What is your fear? If I am late, people will not like me. If I am late, I will get hurt. If I am late, I am not perfect. If I am late that means I am not in control, and that is terrifying. If I am slow, I am not valuable. If I come in last, I am nobody.

If we remove this underlying story—what some like to call a self-limiting belief—the fear and sense of urgency will dissipate. Then we can calmly take steps to remove the obstacles that keep us from being on time, such as trying to do too much in any given time frame. And we can talk to our kids rationally about being responsible citizens, and why they would want to be on time. We can all learn to be punctual for healthy reasons, not because we fear lack of control or self worth.

CHAPTER 13

# The Line

Urgency can drive feelings of insanity. When I feel urgent, I can act like a lunatic. I would never want to watch a video of myself trying to get my daughter out the door in the morning. Although I pride myself on grace, I am pretty sure there is no grace present when I am screaming for her to get out of bed after asking four times with no response.

Where is the line between sanity and insanity? Calm and rage? Love and hatred? Happiness and depression? Courage and fear? Is there really a line at all? Does the line move as we grow in wisdom?

These questions plague me. All I know is that we all have our moments, moments of which we are ashamed and would rather forget. The moment we exploded and yelled at our children. Moments we have replayed in our heads a thousands times wishing we had been our powerful, wise self. Unfortunately, we are human. But humans can choose to see conflict as a gift for the purpose of learning. We can learn to be grateful for those challenging moments since they are opportunities for growth. I am sometimes that type of person, and in others, I start cursing the universe. Never a good idea.

I have seen the sanest people lose their sanity for periods of time. We all have our breaking point, our triggers, our Achilles heel. What is yours? Mine is feeling invisible, unloved or taken advantage of. I brew resentment and then start to behave in ways that are completely out of line with my character. I even watch myself and wonder, what's going on here? It's a sign to look deeper—what am I resenting? My husband is not showing up in our relationship in the way I want? My children are not performing to my desires? I feel as if I have it worse than the rest of the world?

Here's what I think it really is: I try too hard. I give myself away trying to get what I desire. I want more attention, more respect, more help, and more love. My strategy sucks. It doesn't work and leads to all kinds of problems. I end up suffering while those around me enjoy my concierge-like attention and five-star service. They feel great, and I am privately stewing. So why do I stick to a strategy that doesn't work? That's the mystery of humans.

So what do I need to do? I need to speak up and ask for what I want and need—but that scares me. We each have our own childhood dramas that led us to be afraid of asking for what we need, but drama never leads to wisdom. I have to stay focused on my own actions and reactions, and stop blaming others for my internal struggle. I have to admit to myself that speaking up for my needs, wants and desires is not scary. I have made it scary based on events that may or may not have occurred when I was very young.

Little children have no context or wisdom, so the stories they make up about the world are full of holes. Maybe I cried in my crib for longer than I found acceptable, and therefore I decided I could not rely on my parents to meet my needs. Based on a brief moment in time, I developed a lack of trust in other people. Yet, as adults we cling to these stories as truths. Even if we were abused as children, our stories about the world that were birthed by the abuse can continue to plague our adult lives. We must become conscious of these stories and understand them for what they are. They are a child's effort to explain something that makes no sense and should have never occurred. Children do not have the perspective and wisdom to explain why another human would not behave appropriately.

To overcome my fear of speaking up for myself, I started facing other fears, like my fear of heights. I climbed a 50-foot pole in the desert and jumped off to be carried along on a zip line. To say I was terrified is an understatement. I was surrounded by love and the encouragement of strangers struggling with similar fears they were determined to overcome. Before I finally jumped, I was so afraid, I was shaking uncontrollably. I was convinced I would die. Sliding down the zip line, I opened my eyes to the greatest joy I had ever felt. I got to the bottom of the line and received hugs and cheers and congratulations from my friendly, loving strangers and some beautiful friends who sat in 110-degree heat to witness my act of bravery. This moment proved to me I was powerful. The thought of jumping was far worse than actually doing it.

Learning that fear was not reality, I found my voice. I found a way to say things that were scary. And, I did it with as much love as I could muster in my heart. When I came from love, I succeeded.

The danger here is to get attached to the outcome. What if the other person freaks out or does not do what I want them to do? What if they do not come from love? I had to learn to become unattached to the outcome. What I needed for me to be okay was to speak my truth. The result was irrelevant because I know I will be okay no matter what. I have friends who have lost it all and been condemned by the very people who should love them, ostracized by society, and they still stand strong.

Every time I overcome a fear or learn that a trigger is not really a trigger but a sign to pay attention to myself, my line between sanity and insanity moves. My line between calm and rage moves. I become wiser. And that, my friends, is the whole reason we are here.

CHAPTER 14

# Feeling the Pressure to Figure out What to do Next

Nothing brings up your fears and triggers faster than a suffering child. Nothing requires more of your wisdom than coping with such a child.

Every parent has had this feeling—that moment when you must decide what do when your child is sick, suffering or struggling. New parents might experience it when their firstborn has a high fever in the middle of the night. What do you do? Rush to the ER? Wait until morning? Call the doctor?

No one is whispering over your shoulder, "Do this and everything will be okay." It's all on you to come up with a solution to the present dilemma, and if you do not or you come up with the wrong solution, your child may suffer even more. The damage may even be permanent. The child may even die.

WAIT! How did we get here? Notice how quickly I digressed from loving concern to bloody panic?

My wise husband told me, and continues to remind me, that it is not my job to come up with the "brilliant" next step, solution or answer for my son. I continue to watch Joey suffer in pain and writhe in untreatable anxiety regardless of my efforts. All the doctors, therapies and alternative medicines have not seemed to lessen Joey's suffering. We keep trying, and we are always here for him, because we love him.

I have to believe that all of our collective love and efforts have made an enormous difference for Joey. Where would he be if we had not done everything we did? Joey's dad says he believes Joey might have been institutionalized or worse, and Joey's neuropsychiatrist agrees—while I am sobbing over my perceived failures.

One thing I know (I wish I could make this more profound, so please hear it with the resonance I intend): where there is love, there is healing.

Love without wisdom isn't love. Wisdom without love is not wisdom, either. Thanks, Buddha. The tricky part is when we feel the pressure to "figure it out" for our children, we need to stop.

Find a quiet place to calm and clear your mind. Breathe. What comes to you? What knowledge do you have? What do you need? Do you feel clear? There you will find your wisdom. Do you feel love? Then you are on the right track. If you feel fear of any sort, be curious. Where is the fear coming from? Often, parents tell me they are afraid others will judge them as bad parents. Let that go or take that one to your therapist. It does not serve you or your child.

Maybe what those new parents need is some reassurance or even information. So maybe they decide to suck up their pride and call the pediatrician at 3:00AM to ask for advice. Maybe they feel the child is in danger, so they rush to the hospital. Maybe they feel the child will be fine until morning when they call the doctor.

We cannot predict the outcome of our actions regardless of which decision we make. No one can predict the future and to put that kind of pressure on yourself is not wise or healthy. Because of the uncertainty, some people cannot make a decision in these times of stress. They are paralyzed by fear, and that can be very dangerous. Doing nothing—out of fear of doing the wrong thing—is the worst thing. There may be good reasons to choose doing nothing, but fear isn't one of them.

Life is about moving forward. I like to remember Dory from *Finding Nemo* who kept repeating, "Just keep swimming. Just keep swimming." Just keep swimming is my mantra when things are tough. Thank God we live with the dimension of time. We can count on it to continue ticking along, and inevitably, things will be different in the future. How you perceive these things is your choice.

There are families who are faced with tough, heart-wrenching decisions almost daily: anyone who has a child with a psychiatric challenge, a child with ASD, a child who has a chronic illness. If you live with chronic stress and anxiety about your child's condition, my heart is with you. It is not your job to come up with the answer for these children. Love them. Find your clarity and wisdom. Move forward with them. Do not take on the responsibility of the outcome.

Do you really believe that God or the universe expects only perfect, correct answers? How would we learn if not for our mistakes and the chance to try again, only wiser? Give yourself a hug. Consider the possibility this child is a gift to help us grow. I take great comfort in knowing my challenges in life have provided me with wisdom, and, in turn, I have helped others. Without my issues and my children's unbelievable circumstances, I would not have become the person I am today, nor would I have been able to touch the hearts of so many people. Existentially, I know why I am here.

By now you know my belief that the meaning of life is to grow, learn and become one with the love of the universe, God, or whatever you want to call it, that exists within each and every one of us. We all have our unique lesson plan for our time in Earth school. My great teacher, Kimberly, says, "We have two choices, love or fear." The choice is obvious—however, not always the easiest to make. I encourage all parents to choose love. Fear is confusing and can paralyze us. Parents need clarity and wisdom more than anything, especially when faced with a child who is suffering or is ill. Clarity and wisdom are never found under the shroud of fear. Fear's real purpose is to lead us to learning and enlightenment. When I look at the cause of my fear, I can grow and become wiser and clearer.

Fear can be a great teacher. When fear rears its ugly head, pay attention to what it is telling you and do your work and move back into love. Your children need you. They thrive when you are coming from love. If you are afraid, they will be afraid, and no parent wants that for their child.

CHAPTER 15

# Hope can be a Bitch

Here is something else we want for our children, although this one is a trap: Success. We hope for it with our whole being and this hope typically comes from fear. Hope can be a bitch.

When you are rooting with all your heart for your kid to do well and for things to go his way—stop! It's a set-up. Realize it for what it is: you wanting to feel better.

I sat in the Atlanta airport on my way home from a weeklong stay at my university. I was relaxed and connected with my life purpose. I felt strong and at peace, ready to go back to my real life. I had learned so much. One of my instructors warned us that we would be tested as we transitioned back into our lives, some of us even in the airport. I guess I was one of the lucky ones.

I was excited to hear from my oldest son's father that Joey had decided to try to take the ACT. He actually went to the building with pencils and calculator in hand along with that crazy piece of paper with your picture on it so you do not send in a ringer to ace your ACT.

To put this monumental event into context, Joey is a brilliant child who has struggled since the day he entered preschool. He has at least eight formal diagnoses including but not limited to dysgraphia, anxiety, school-related anxiety and depression, Ehlers-Danlos Syndrome, dyscalculia, AD/HD Inattentive Type, developmental disorders, sensory processing dysfunction, autoimmune problems and a few others.

I anxiously awaited any news from Joey's dad about how things went. I was hopeful! Then I got the text. Joey finished filling out his name and the demographic information. Then he sat there for three hours staring at his test. Just staring.

All of the joy and hope in my heart was released in the Atlanta airport with an audible "Nooooo!!!!!" that echoed down the massive corridor for what seemed like minutes.

People stared at me.

I curled up in the fetal position and felt like my heart had been torn in two, as it had been so many times. We had worked so hard to make it to this moment. Joey is so smart. He could ace that test if I was reading it to him and filling in the bubbles for him. I had dragged this poor boy through school up until this point. He was beaten and ragged and exhausted and sicker than I ever imagined.

He had frozen on important exams before and suffered for it. He was forced to retake Algebra and Geometry in high school because he could not take the placement exam. He just stared at those, too. He is brilliant at math, he just cannot write. He needs a scribe, and he has to trust that scribe. Joey was bored out of his mind retaking these courses. The teachers in the high school said he was the smartest kid they had ever had in class, and he continually asked questions that left even the teacher in the dust.

My favorite story about Joey and math is when he came home in third grade and told his MIT math major father that his teacher did not agree with him when he told her there were an infinite number of points between any two points on the number line. Ugh.

When we finally showed Joey some mercy and allowed him to be homebound the last quarter of his junior year in high school, he had a tutor for each class come to the house. He was taking trigonometry. The tutor was a sweet young woman who was preparing to teach math at the high school level. Boy was she delighted when within five minutes, Joey was teaching her trigonometry she had since forgotten from college. She repeatedly told us she thought it was ridiculous they were forcing Joey to do so many problems when he obviously understood all of this material better than most teachers.

So there I was in the Atlanta airport, tears running down my cheeks, defeated, again. Was there no mercy? Couldn't we get a break, just once? Joey deserved so much more. Poor Joey. Poor me.

But Joey was actually just fine after the ACT disaster. He learned that he really needed a reader and needed to take the test over multiple days. In the end, the school counselor and I worked to get this accommodation for Joey, and he did eventually complete the ACT and got a decent score. So what was really going on with me in that airport?

I wanted to feel better because I was tired of holding all of the emotional pain around my son's challenges. I was looking to feel better. I wanted some validation that all of the sacrifices and lost hours of my life working tirelessly by his side were going to "pay off" in the traditional sense. I was holding on to Joey taking the ACT so I could have something I could hold up to the world and say, "See! He is okay! Therefore, I am okay! Now I can feel better!"

I see this faulty thought pattern quite a bit with parents regardless of the challenges their child is facing. It has nothing to do with the child or their issues. It is about the parent wanting to feel better about themselves. They are holding on to the idea that their children will perform in some way. Get that A. Earn that spot on the team. Score that goal. Win that trophy. Get into that university. Why? Not because they want their kids to be happy—that answer is a convenient and acceptable distraction from the painful reality no one wants to admit. All parents want their kids to be happy, but we're more complex and messed-up than we realize. Parents want to feel better. They are seeking fulfillment and joy, not just for their children, but for themselves. There is nothing like the feeling of watching your child win or achieve. But when it comes from a selfish place, it's like a drug, and it can be harmful to your child.

I admit it—I selfishly wanted to feel better about Joey's situation. I was tired and battered and worn, worse than he was. I feared the future more than he did because I had lived it. I was not giving Joey credit for being capable or creative or resourceful or even resilient. He is probably the most resilient child I have ever met. So, why do I feel so much pain when he has a setback?

I am enmeshed. I can only be okay if he is okay. That's a powerless position to be in. It's codependence, and it puts too much pressure on a child.

Even worse—Joey has carried the burden of my worry for years. He worries about me, because he loves me. He knows if he is okay, then I am happy. It's a trap! Neither of us will ever feel okay until one of us lets go of the rope and trusts that the other one will be okay on their own. It's a kind of standoff. We both love each other. How could either of us let go of the emotional rope we've both been clinging to like a lifeline?

I am the adult. I am the one with more wisdom. I know if I let go, he will be free of being emotionally responsible for me and free to find his own way in the world. This is the hardest thing I've ever had to do, and that's saying something given the path I have followed. I needed to let go emotionally of carrying Joey through life. He needed to learn how to function on his own. I remind myself daily to let go. (There should be a group for Enmeshment Anonymous!) When I start to hope on behalf of Joey, I stop, breathe and realize how wonderful he is, just the way he is. I would not want someone to believe I was/am incapable. That would piss me off to no end. So, how could I do that to my own child, no matter what his challenge?

All children, no matter what their situation, deserve a life filled with love and healthy support devoid of judgment. They deserve parents who celebrate their failures with them as their greatest learning opportunities. We can commend our children for their effort, not their grades, trophies, or pieces of paper (thank you Carol Dweck for your research). Praise effort, not outcomes. We cannot control outcomes—grades and college admissions are subjective. Not making the team might have meant having a bad day. Since we can't control outcomes, we need to stop hoping on behalf of our children. Empower them to put forth their best effort. Shower them with your wisdom about making choices that are good for them and in line with their true life purpose.

And if you still feel awful whenever your child has a setback, find someone to help you work through the pain. It has little to do with your child. Our kids are just holding up the mirror so we can identify what we need to be working on.

That day in the Atlanta airport, I was reminded that I no longer need to prove myself to anyone. Test scores do not define me. Following my passion and life purpose, which is to help others find their way, means everything. Help your children find their passion—or at least be aware enough to know passion when it comes along.

CHAPTER 16

# *What's in a Grade?*

Speaking of hope, how often have you hoped while opening the report card or the letter from that college?

Our children, especially our teens, put such effort into school these days. Even if they are not gunning for Harvard or getting straight A's in AP classes, they are putting forth effort in a way no working adult would tolerate. Most adults would find it unacceptable to go to work all day and then be required to do hours of work at night as well. Unions would be in an uproar. We would scream about the importance of rest and leisure and quality time with the family.

I witnessed my freshman in high school work so very hard for a C in his English class. I even wrote an essay for him to test whether the teacher had a bias against him or not. I wrote a fine essay. I got a C. In my mind, I was thinking, "Really?!?"

This reminds me of my children's father's favorite story of sticking it to a high school teacher. He and a friend suspected that their English teacher was not actually reading their work objectively but giving a grade based on reputation. Ken was a genius and his friend (let's call him Danny) was "not a genius." So they turned in the same paper, completely identical. Ken got his typical A. Danny got his typical C. They presented their case to the school board. All they got was some personal satisfaction.

Today I was in a manic "I must throw away everything in the house" state of mind. So, I went into "the pantry," the resting place for everything in life we do not know what to do with. (I know I should not end a sentence with a preposition. It is satisfying for me to send a "F-You" into the universe every now and then so my past composition teachers can feel my dyslexic rage.)

I pulled out a stack of papers about two feet high. I was about to exchange this stack of papers for a single paper with six critical letters printed on it. This piece of paper was a report card. The two foot high stack of papers represented painfully completed US History worksheets and maps (beautifully colored by me because my 17-year-old cannot hold a colored pencil let alone manipulate it), AP Composition papers, pre-calculus problems, physics labs, Spanish translations, PE tests (Isn't the point of PE to get exercise? Why are they wasting time taking tests?), and, God help me, reflections on how you feel religion has helped you in your life. This pile represented hundreds of hours of my son sitting in class sweating his balls off.

(I got a phone call one day from the Dean of Joey's non-air-conditioned Catholic high school. She said, "Joe needs to tell you something." Joe gets on the line and says, "Mom, I am sweating my balls off, and I can't take it any more. Come get me." I don't know if the humor is coming through here, but it was hilarious at the time.)

So this stack of papers…the effort, the money, the time, the anxiety, the therapy…it represented a miracle as far as Joey was concerned. And for what? A letter on a piece of paper. Honors Physics Lab: B.

Imagine the next time you open your paycheck and for six months worth of work, instead of a check for money, you receive a piece of paper and all that is written on it is a B. There is your reward for six months. A ridiculously simplistic "B" written on a piece of paper.

Ponder this for a while. I think it violates some child labor law.

We need to keep it in perspective. Do you or your children fear the grades they will receive? If this is true, then there is no safety for learning to occur. I have had a number of parents tell me it is unacceptable for any of their children to receive a letter grade less than a B. God help those kids if they ever meet up with my engineering calculus teacher from my freshman year of college. I prayed daily for a C. It was my first C, and I was never more relieved or proud of myself. What mattered was that I never gave up, and I put forth effort. So, I would love to pull out those parent's report cards who do not "accept" lower grades. I think it might become obvious why they have such lofty expectations. Either they found school very easy and have no empathy for those who struggle, or they did not meet someone else's unrealistic expectation and are trying to insulate themselves from reliving that pain.

In any case, we need to think carefully about how much we pressure our children to get those grades. Are they that important? Let's make sure we're not pressuring them so that we can feel good about ourselves.

I threw the 1000 pieces of paper away and taped the one piece of paper with the six letters on it to the fridge, breathing a huge sigh of relief.

CHAPTER 17

# Invisible Disabilities and Outliers

Grades are stressors for all families. However, if you have a learning disabled or just one of those mystery kids (Joey was labeled a mystery in grade school. Really helpful!), grades can be the fuel for divorce, abuse, and serious psychiatric problems for everyone in the family.

So what do you do when you have one of these outlier kids? I think Charles Schulz was brilliant when he said in one of his Peanuts comic strips that education is like bowling. "You throw a ball down the middle and hope to hit a few pins on the ends." If your child is one of the pins on the side—it doesn't matter which side, gifted or delayed or both—then you know what I mean. Some of you may even have a pin two lanes over—and then what?

How can we expect an educational system designed for the masses to handle every anomaly that comes along? It's impossible. Having sat on the Board of Trustees of a private school and having kids in public and private schools for the last 17 years, I have seen quite a bit. I have counseled a number of families with unique children. These kids do not fit in well, anywhere.

Another category of child that creates waves is the one with the invisible disability:

The girl with AD/HD, Inattentive Type.

The boy who is having seizures that no one can recognize.

The child who is brilliant but cannot write a sentence to save his life.

The teenager suffering from debilitating anxiety no one understands because she has masked it with high performance and perfectionism.

Dyscalculia, dysgraphia, AD/HD, anxiety, emotional challenges, trauma, dyslexia, sensory processing dysfunction, expressive and receptive language disorders in intelligent children—these are just a few of the invisible disabilities that are dangerous beyond their own characteristics.

To be intelligent and dyslexic is torture. I am speaking from experience—no one knew I could not read easily. I did not even realize my struggle until I was considering going to law school. I could not read one page in the time it took my classmates to read an entire case study. I graduated from college with honors and studied abroad at Cambridge. I was salutatorian in my high school. (I would have been valedictorian had it not been for my ruptured appendix in March of my senior year. My biology teacher insisted I take all the tests I missed on the day I returned to school after being out for almost an entire quarter. I still think he is a jerk. Amazing what we never let go of.) I was obviously intelligent and capable, but dyslexia slammed door after door in my face, and I can still hear the ringing in my ears.

I changed my major from biomedical engineering to economics because too many of the teaching assistants in engineering did not speak English well, and I depended on learning in class because I could not read the textbook. I knew I was in trouble when my chemistry lab instructor spoke almost no English and told us to read the book and the labs. He could not even answer my questions. Economics did not require much reading. It was mostly common sense and statistics to me. I graduated with honors from the College of Business, having written a 50-page thesis on the European Economic Community and its effects on agriculture.

How did I do it? Sheer stubbornness and persistence. It took me forever. I did not eat or sleep much, and I gave up drinking, at least for that year of school.

No one knew the extent of my disability. All they saw was my intellect and what I had produced. No one ever considered I might not be living up to my potential because what I was producing was above average and seen as stellar by everyone.

I knew.

And it killed my self-esteem. I would search for validation anywhere I could find it. I had no idea how to ask for help, which I saw as a sign of weakness. I could not let anyone know I was struggling, because I might shatter the illusion of my identity as the smart kid. It was all I had. So, I had a plan. If I ever failed, I would kill myself. Simple, elegant. Only, there was a problem. My mom told me once when I was a little girl that only selfish people kill themselves. I do not completely agree given my current knowledge of neuroscience and psychology; however, this sentence she had implanted in my brain at a critical age kept me alive. I was not selfish. If anything, I was a giver. I wanted to rescue the world (not necessarily a healthy goal, but it kept me alive).

I lived in anxiety and shame. Self-judgment. It's a horrible thing. If I could rid the world of one thing, it would be self-judgment. To tell yourself over and over again, day after day, that you are unlovable, unworthy, or a failure, is a hell that no one should experience. But all too many gifted people live in this secret world of self-judgment. They know they are not living up to their potential because of their hidden disabilities and challenges that no one has identified (maybe not even they themselves). Even the most successful and famous people secretly torture themselves with self-judgment. None of us is immune.

These outliers and secretly disabled children need our support. Parents, here is your opportunity to shine. Seek to understand your children. See them clearly as they are, not as you wish them to be. Accept them. And find help. Advocate for them and teach them to advocate for themselves, because believe it or not, you cannot go to high school or college with them. Remind teachers. Learn how to have collaborative conversations with educators so they understand. I have had more success having a short meeting with a teacher at the beginning of the year briefly explaining exactly what my son needed in her class to be successful than any two hour IEP (Individualized Education Plan) meeting I have ever attended. Most teachers are great people who want to be good at what they do. Even the best teacher cannot know how to reach every child. They need your help. Collaborate with them and always, always bring chocolate or donuts to the meeting. It is the white flag to take them off of the defensive.

Too many parents have come to me, deeply angry with their children's schools and teachers. They seem to believe the school or teacher is out to get their child. While my husband has shared many stories with me of growing up in southwest Iowa and the beatings he took from peers and humiliation he suffered inflicted by teachers, I still believe that these people who seemed evil and ill-intended were ignorant and suffering themselves. They believed my husband was different and willfully defiant. They judged him. And we know when people judge others it is because they are hurting inside and do not like to look at their own shortcomings. Someone who hates feminine men probably fears his or her own femininity or masculinity, and what it means about them. Bullies who hurt people know no other way to manage their own pain than to lash out at others. Maybe it's the only thing they have ever seen at home.

Stop judging and getting angry with your schools and your children's teachers. Offer them some compassion. See them as creative, resourceful and whole. Offer to partner with them by providing your understanding of your child. Be open and listen to their observations and suggestions. Accept their limitations. You just might learn something from them. Teachers observe a lot of children and, in my experience, are often the ones who can flag a child who is struggling. They are also a little more detached than you as a parent.

Try not to bring any more drama to your child's situation than necessary. Resist the dark side and stand in love. You will get so much more out of your schools and teachers when you do. Trust me on this one.

I work to diffuse drama all of the time, especially with my kids. Kelly tells me her history teacher "hates" her. I talked to her history teacher, and he loves Kelly! He said the world needs more Kellys. She is brilliant and has opinions and enthusiasm and shares her endless information with the class. What she is sensing is not his hatred but his frustration with her impulsivity. He still has to teach all the kids in the class, and, with a firecracker like Kelly in the mix, well, let's just say she does not make a teacher's job easy. So I do not respond to Kelly's dramatic interpretation of her history teacher's momentary frustrations. I re-frame over and over again for her what is really going on so her ruminations do not consume her.

If your child says their teacher hates them, talk to the teacher. I guarantee you will be surprised by what you hear. And if the teacher actually confirms they hate your child, write to me, I want to hear about the context of the situation. And then remove your child from that class or school.

Your outlier or disabled child has great potential, and a school may or may not be able to tap that potential. You have to be okay with that. Help can be found in all kinds of creative places. The world needs these kids who live outside the box. This is where innovation and invention come from!

CHAPTER 18

# School Haters

So now that we have broached the topic of kids who are not school friendly...

Parents can generally be divided into two groups: those who look forward to school starting again in the fall and those who dread it with every bone in their body. You know immediately who you are.

Some of you are probably being driven crazy by the kids who have taken to annoying the crap out of each other or you. Annoying the crap out of someone should be an Olympic sport. My teenage boy might be a medal contender. He has a particular gift for knowing exactly when to target his victim. He has the tenacity of a termite and the verbal finesse that Mark Twain would envy. No, change that to Truman Capote. (By the way, the only reason I know anything about Truman Capote is because I had to read aloud one of his books to Joey. It was gruesome.)

The worst part is he takes a sick pleasure in watching his sisters scream in rage at his taunts. It is really something to watch. He is a true master. The beautiful part of watching him work his craft is that when confronted, he will act as if he did absolutely nothing to create the fallout that has occurred. Effortless, something to behold. Almost a reason to start drinking again.

No wonder so many parents love the smell of sharpened pencils in the fall. (And excuse me, but fall does not start until the end of September so when did school ever start in the fall?) It means a break from the never-ending demands of children.

However, there is a group of parents, and I think there are more of us than we might guess, who secretly dread school. Those parents of kids with AD/HD, those parents whose children are targets for bullying, those parents whose children are learning disabled and are not having their needs met, those parents whose children who suffer from anxiety—the list goes on and on. Those parents are saying prayers at night or making deals with a God they may or may not believe in.

"If John has a more understanding teacher this year, I promise I will finally clean out the garage," or whatever ridiculous promise you come up with in the moment. My personal favorite is when I promise to never yell at my kids again. Good Lord! That lasts about eight hours.

Having a child with a disability or a learning challenge or a social or emotional issue can create upheaval in a parent's life. My son's neurobehavioral psychologist looked at his profile and said, "I am surprised you are still married." I groaned. Joey's dad and I had just divorced, but we were both there in support of our son. She went on to explain that most relationships do not survive such a challenge. While I do not know of any research that says the divorce rate of challenging children is higher than that of easy children, I can only speak from my personal experience. My four children have functioned as a magnifying glass focusing on my own issues and me. I have always known I was an impatient person. In fact, I prayed for patience when I was a little girl. What a fool I was!

I got a graduate course in patience. I got four kids who test me hourly so I can practice patience.

My first child did not sleep through the night until he was five years old. Not five months—five years. Kelly refused to wear underwear until she was 10. She still refuses socks and coats. She skis with no socks. Jackie asks the same question sometimes forty times in a day and insists on packing for vacations a month in advance. Tommy continues to push everyone's buttons and is clueless to his real impact.

So I dread the start of school. My blood pressure skyrockets as I consider the never-ending hours of scribing for Joey, the tears, the anxiety, the guilt and stress, the lost homework, the poor grades despite an encyclopedic knowledge of the subject, the behavior disasters, the lost years of learning due to teachers who refused accommodations or just did not get it.

So, if you are one who secretly hates "school" on behalf of your kids and the strained relationships and difficult home life, you are not alone. My recommendation is to shift the focus in your family, because there is more to life than school. What does your child do well? What are her strengths? Is your home a happy one? If it is not, focus on how to make it happy. Shift the conversations away from school, which is something you cannot control. Do you and your kids laugh together? Play games? Watch movies? Go on outings?

Try not to let school bleed into every other aspect of life. I've had to work very hard to learn to laugh again with my children who struggle enormously with school. I am vigilant about finding ways to enjoy being a family (strangely, we all seem to love Steve Harvey and *Family Feud*—who knew?) It is not easy but it is the only way to prove to your children they are more important and significant than whatever is going on in school.

CHAPTER 19

# Clues to Reality

Behavior.

Difficult to manage behavior can make any child or parent detest school. However, unlike homework, the topic of behavior is deeply complex and incredibly important, and there's more to it than simply controlling it.

Behavior can be like grabbing a badger. You do not want to deal with it because it looks and feels unpleasant and when you finally do go after it, you realize it is completely unpredictable and downright nasty. Toddlers are exhausting with their endless testing this behavior and that behavior. So are teenagers. Behavior is even more ominous when it occurs in the classroom.

When I say the word behavior, many parents have an immediate negative reaction. Technically, behavior is a neutral word. And to take this a bit further, both good behavior and bad behavior can tell parents what is going on with their children. I have to be honest. My 16-year-old son brought me roses the other day out of the blue. The first thing that ran through my head was, "What did he do?" Good psychologists can tell as much from good behavior as bad behavior. Behavior is an outward clue as to what is going on internally with your child.

I'm not asking you to become Sherlock here. Sherlock was famous for deductive reasoning, but with human behavior, we can only do our best with inductive reasoning which provides us with our best guess as to what's going on.

Many parents make the mistake of assuming their child will tell them when something is bothering them emotionally. Ahem. Kids typically don't think, "Oh, I should share this with Mom."

"Hey, Mom! My core shame around being unlovable has cropped up again, because I did not get an A on my last history test. I have noticed that my perfectionism in response to what I have perceived as an identity failure has been on the rise along with my anxiety. I recognize my need to be impossibly perfect is planting seeds of self-hatred. We should really talk about this."

If only it was that easy.

I have to share this story. It is kind of relevant because it is about behavior, and it is just funny. My daughter Kelly, when she was about five years old, liked to be naked. She had sensory issues regarding clothes against her skin, but we believe she also grew to enjoy the attention it brought her. So, we were driving to Myrtle Beach, the annual family reunion location, and, of course, we passed some strip joints along the way. Kelly, being annoyingly observant, noticed a sign that said exotic dancers. She asked what an "exotic dancer store" was. Her dad explained that it was a place where adults could watch women dance with no clothes on, giving it as little energy as possible knowing the boys would blurt something from *South Park* if he did not give an acceptable answer. Kelly then responded, "Maybe I could work there someday! I like to dance, and I like to be naked!" Her brothers laughed for the rest of the car ride. Kelly was pleased with herself.

Using my inductive reasoning, I know that Kelly's argumentative nature and her outbursts in school are due in part to her extreme sensory issues and her epilepsy. Her emotional brain is always is in a state of overwhelm.

You can relate. Have you ever worked out in the heat for a long period of time or ran a marathon or just had an exhausting day? Try doing calculus afterwards or even balancing your checkbook. You can become a little testy. You can't focus because you're hot and all you want is a shower. Kelly is like that all day, everyday. It is hard for her to live in her own skin. We cannot "see" this, but I can use her behavior as a clue. She can't tolerate certain smells (her least favorite is oranges—go figure). She hates it when someone is listening to the TV at a normal sound level. She claims it is too loud. However, when she is watching, the TV is deafening, and she is just fine. She hates to wear clothes. We have spent thousands of dollars trying to find clothes she might be willing to wear. Most are passed on to needy children unworn. She spent her toddler years naked. I would dress her and then a minute later she would be streaking through the house. She did have a Band-Aid fetish though. Too bad they did not make clothes out of Band-Aids.

Now that she is in high school, she can't stand people. They are all stupid. She says she has no desire to fit in; however, she joined the robotics team. That tells me she does have an underlying desire to find her people. When you are as out-of-the-box as Kelly in terms of intelligence and issues, it is difficult to find your people. It took me 43 years to find my people, and they are rare indeed.

So, back to behavior. When behavior takes an ugly turn, try not to judge your child. View the behavior through the detective's magnifying glass. What is that behavior telling you? Is the behavior new? Is it out of character? Talk to your child without leading the witness; meaning, don't assume they are just being bad. Bing Crosby said in *The Bells of*

*Saint Mary's*, "There is no such thing as a bad boy." I agree with Bing wholeheartedly. There is always a reason behind behavior.

Joey was born a happy little guy despite his sensory problems and his terrible vision and chronic pain and his constant need for my presence. When Joey was in a comfortable environment, he was happy. That was his norm. So, we should have been wiser when we saw the happy Joey transform into the fetal position Joey by fourth grade. When we received the diagnosis of school-related anxiety and depression, I knew I should have followed my gut and pulled him out of school sooner.

My second son, Tommy, was the funny love bug of the family. He was always cuddling and always trying to make everyone laugh. So, in third grade when he started saying he was fat (in reality, he was quite thin), and he did not like himself, I was a little wiser, a little faster than I was with Joey. Tommy has an expressive and receptive language disorder that did not become obvious until third grade, which is usually the year when learning disabilities start to become more evident. His behavior was not him but a reflection of his frustration about not being able to function in school at his true potential. We found him the support he needed after doing some extensive investigating.

Behavior is a clue to a child's underlying struggle. An anxious child is rarely "just" anxious. I always look for a cause. I came out of the womb anxious due to a genetic disorder, so I do not always need an additional reason to be anxious. I've had to learn how to calm myself despite my normal state of vigilance. However, anxiety builds more anxiety. So, I must remain ever watchful for things that might be aggravating my anxiety.

Here is a different way to consider behavior. How many times have you fought with your partner or friend when, in actuality, you know deep down inside that you are fighting because you are upset about something completely different. I will start to pick a fight with my husband when I am upset about one of the children just so I do not have to feel that pain. It sounds nuts, but we all do it.

The wisdom to be found here is that we need to stop addressing behavior in isolation. Punishment, reward and neglect are typically not effective approaches to managing behavior. I have had no success with these approaches. Predetermined consequences for older children work very well. When Tommy violates a rule, he knows exactly what will happen. We have it documented in a contract. When he is creative enough to come up with a whopper that is not documented, Dad and I have a conference to determine how to amend the contract. I highly recommend Dr. Daniel Siegel's book, *The Whole-Brain Child*, to figure out how to discipline and interact with your child.

We must understand that behavior is a clue to the mysterious brain, emotions, health and mind of a person. So, next time your child acts out, ask yourself why. You might find yourself less reactive and a tad more curious, which is good for you and your child. And you might not be so worried when your daughter says she might aspire to dance naked for a living.

CHAPTER 20

# Pluto is No Longer Labeled a Planet.

When we have a child struggling with behavior, learning, or thriving, we in the Western world have an immediate desire to label it, to figure out what to call it.

Labels are created by people in a moment of time with the best intention and knowledge that is available at that specific time. Even in the course of my children's lives, the oldest now being 19, they have been labeled and relabeled and relabeled and relabeled. Parents are driven to find out "what" their children have, but they miss what is staring them in the face every morning. It's as if that label was the Holy Grail. If we can just figure out what little Johnny has, then we can all sleep better at night. Maybe it's because we believe that if we label a child AD/HD or dyslexic, it takes the blame and finger-pointing away from us and redirects them toward the label.

My children and I have been awarded lots of labels. The labels have never been the Holy Grail. They have never helped me cope as a parent or as a labeled person myself. In some moments, new labels have shown me how damaging the previous labels were because the medication used to treat label #1 made label #2 worse. Talk about feeling awful. I trusted these doctors to know what they were doing. I believed some of them when they said they could help my child. Sometimes I would get caught in the "This is it!" trap. I have been disappointed every time. I have heard stories about people who go to psychiatrists and doctors and receive a diagnosis and a treatment and their condition improves or is even "cured."

There is no cure for my children, but I will not cease to work with both Western and Eastern medicine. My acquired wisdom has taught me to listen to doctors and trust my intuition. I am open. And I know, the hard way, that the label handed us today will absolutely change as our understanding of the brain and body expands. No different than Pluto, my children may no longer be labeled planets tomorrow. It is my prediction Pluto, now considered a dwarf planet, will receive another new label someday along with the rest of us.

Like our comprehension of the universe, our understanding of the functions of genes, the brain, and the body is in its infancy.

As a parent, do the best you can with the doctors and therapists you are working with and know that they are human with limited access to the complete understanding of your child. Remember it was not that long ago doctors were using leeches and bleeding people.

If you are putting most of your energy into seeking the Holy Grail, take a moment to assess whether some of that energy needs to be redirected to either caring for yourself or for your suffering child. You have the best chance, even without a PhD, to help your child thrive. Your love and guidance is what they really need—not a label.

CHAPTER 21

# *Beautiful*

Beautiful is one label I love.

Being dyslexic, I had a horrid time learning how to spell words. There are particular words that I give more importance to than others, so those words demand extra effort on my part. The word "beautiful" is one of those words. I think I reliably remembered how to spell it by seventh grade or sometime around then. The word even sounds beautiful. When people apply beautiful to you in any context it makes you feel amazing. I still internally squeal with delight when my husband tells me I am beautiful, or that I have a beautiful heart.

I think we all should use the word beautiful as many times as possible with our daughters before they move out of the house. It's especially critical for girls to hear it from the father figure in the house. A young girl needs to hear how beautiful she is, and yes, every girl is beautiful exactly as she is.

I am not exactly sure if my father ever looked me in the eye and told me I was a beautiful person. The only thing I remember was my dad pointing out that I had gained a few pounds in high school. He said, "You might want to lay off on the cheeseburgers at the McDonald's drive-through."

I was crushed. It lingers with me, thirty-five years later. In that moment, I learned it was not okay to gain weight.

Words are powerful. Words linger with us even if the other person forgets them the moment they leave their lips. Let your words linger in a beautiful way.

CHAPTER 22

# "Because I said so…"

Talk about lingering words! These words still echo in my head from my childhood.

Many parents tell me their kids should behave in a certain way because parents are the authority figures. When we were kids and challenged our parents with the infamous, "Why?" they simply responded, "Because I said so." I certainly never challenged my parents. That was a boundary I didn't dare cross.

Why doesn't "because I said so" work any more?

My mom could stare down an angry bull without a word and, in a moment, instill the fear of God in someone. My dad would make a subtle gesture towards his belt buckle that sent us bolting towards the closest exit.

My kids respond with demands of explanation, and, as if we were in a court of law, retort a long list of precedents establishing case law that refutes my logic. The little demons are usually right which is even more irritating. My kids can point out every moment in history when I did not hold a boundary and let them do the very thing I am asking them not to do (e.g. eat cupcakes before bed).

I tried "the look" one day and got in return, "Mom, are you okay? Do you have to go to the bathroom?"

My favorite issue between my kids and me is swearing. I swear. A LOT. It is part of who I am. I come from master linguists who consider swearing a higher form of communication. I still think that scene from *A Christmas Story* is hilarious when Ralphy said his father wove a tapestry of profanity that is still hovering over Indiana. If that is possible, my family might be in large part responsible for global warming.

Still, when my pretty 14-year-old girl starts dropping F-bombs for rhetorical emphasis, I say, "Don't swear, it is unbecoming." Yes, I hear the words coming out of my mouth and feel the hypocrisy course through my veins. She does not experience shame or remorse; she exploits the opportunity to practice her litigation skills. "Mom, you swear all the time." She pauses for emphasis. "Really!"

Be the change you want to see in the world. Thanks, Gandhi.

CHAPTER 23

# Requests Versus Complaints

Here is another change in the parent/child relationship that differs from when I was a kid. I am convinced there is a whoopee cushion on the couch that instead of fart noises spews, "Moooommmmm!!!" because every time my ass hits that couch, that's what I hear. Typically followed by, "I'm hungry!"

Now, think about it. "I am hungry" is a statement of one's condition. Because my children believe me to be both psychic and omnipotent, the statement is followed by silence. Now, if I were to enter into a restaurant, sit down at a table and before the server could make their way over to the table, shout, "I AM HUNGRY!" this person who is getting paid would look at me like I was a complete jerk. I'm not telling the server what I want from the menu. I didn't even look at the menu. I feel so entitled and kingly that just my proclamation should be enough for the server to run into the kitchen and prepare me exactly what I want to eat. God help the poor slob if they bring me something I do not like or liked yesterday but have decided I no longer like today.

This scenario goes on in homes around the country everyday, and we do not hesitate to act on command. What kind of message are we sending our children? If mom is serving the princes and princesses of the abode, then they are learning that they need not be kind or respectful, especially toward women. Girls are going to believe it will be their job to serve their families in the same manner. Boys will have an expectation that they can shout out their complaint and expect their wife to magically solve it. I know many women who also carry the emotional burden for the entire household because that is what their mothers did.

Let's end this right now. We are not psychic nor are we servants. We work hard and deserve the respect of everyone in our household just as we should respect them. It doesn't take much to tweak a complaint into a polite request. Next time you hear, "I'm hungry!" or my personal pet peeve, "I'm bored!" ask them to reframe their complaint into a request. Seriously, we have more entertainment and food in our household than a small country. When I was a kid and we said we were bored, my parents sent us out to hoe weeds and water plants in the nursery. So, we quickly learned to never say we were bored. Depending on your kid's age, reframe the complaint to something resembling, "Mom, I am hungry, could you help me make a sandwich?" Or "Dad, I am hungry, do you mind if I make myself a salad since dinner is two hours away?" If the child or teen is capable of making their own food, encourage them to get it for themselves. Help them to learn to care for themselves.

This sense of independence will go a long way in helping them to thrive when they go off into the real world. I have an 18-year-old who cannot pour himself a glass of water due to some serious motor skill and vision problems. So, I get it. But I've done him a disservice by not being patient and working with him on this task. Maybe it would take us a week to master it, but he could do it if I was persistent enough. I'm not though, because I have too many children, and I am exhausted and overwhelmed. I get it.

So, now, as he graduates high school, he cannot go off to college like his peers despite his brilliance. He is incapable of caring for himself and does not believe he is capable. We will spend the next year teaching him life skills he should have learned along the way but did not, because I did everything for him. I missed that line in the sand when I should have encouraged him to try instead of enabling him to stay dependent. I am not sure when that moment in time occurred, but it did, and I wasn't even looking for it.

We always have to be vigilant in noticing what our children are capable of doing on their own. We wouldn't ask a 2-year-old to cross the street alone, but I might have asked Joey to try to pour his own water when he turned 12 so he could practice. Maybe at 18 he would have mastered it. Who cares about the spills and broken cups? What matters is that Joey believes he is capable. Right now, he does not. And that is, in part, my fault.

It is emotionally heart wrenching to watch your child suffer from anxiety or low self-esteem. It can trigger all kinds of trauma within us. As adults, we need to be strong and wise on behalf of our children. Seek the support you need to work on your own challenges, and for the sake of your child, empower them by teaching them how to care for themselves, how to solve their own problems, and how to be in a respectful relationship with another human.

Encourage clear communication. If the child is complaining, ask them to request something specific. This is forcing them to consider what they really want and need. Many adults cannot even do this for themselves. They rely on their spouse to make all their decisions for them. It is disturbing to observe when you know what you're looking at. I see my relatives (I'm not being specific, so I am not completely excommunicated) look to their spouse to wait on them hand and foot or to make even the most trivial decisions including what they want for dinner or what they will wear. Codependence is unsettling.

Do not respond to a complaint until it is turned into a request, and do not prompt the kids when they get older. "Mom, I'm hungry, can you get me something to eat?" "Sure, honey, what do you want?" "I don't know, what do you have?" Ah! They've tricked you into solving their dilemma again. Have them get up and go into the kitchen and look in the fridge or pantry and decide what they want, just like I have to read the menu at a restaurant. When they decide on their own, you can decide if they are capable of handling it themselves and if not, whether you're willing to assist.

My teenage boys love to ask for food at 11:00 p.m. after all the dishes are done, the food is put away, and I'm just about to walk upstairs to collapse into bed. What is that all about? Previously, I caved and made them food. I even listed every option I could think of in the middle of my cognitive exhaustion. They never considered me or my need for sleep. (And I have a real medical need for sleep. My brain is sick, and sleep is the primary cure.) Still, I set aside my own personal health to enable my sons' entitlement. I am not getting paid, so I am pretty sure that made me their servant. Ugh!

I have learned to say no to them without the pang of guilt I once felt. I am honest and say I need to sleep now. You are on your own. They need to be able to find their way out of that maze. What will they do once I am gone? God forbid if they treat their wives that way.

I was surprised by their response. They did not whine or complain. They simply said, "Okay," and went on—either without food or by getting something themselves. I should have started working on this one at a much younger age. My husband did with his son at a young age. My stepson forgets every now and then, but my husband remains vigilant. My three stepsons are the most polite children you will ever meet. He makes me look really bad sometimes (it's annoying).

The other problem with allowing our children to complain without making a clear request is that they might not actually get their need met. I hear, "I hate school," a lot. But what I do not hear is a clear request because children are not often required to be specific. Parents instantly go into solving mode. "Why do you hate school? Is it your teacher? Is someone bullying you? Are you having trouble in math?"

Instead of putting the effort (and yes, it takes effort) into trying to do some soul searching as to what the source of their hatred of school is, they will typically pick one of the things you just listed for them. "Yeah, I hate math." It's easy. They're secretly hoping you'll let them stay home from school or something along those lines. If you wait without prompting them, you might get something that would give you a real clue as to the source of their hatred.

"Kids on the playground are jerks." Your response might be, "Say more about that." See how far you can get before you intervene. Even go so far as to ask them how they think they should go about resolving the problem. Guide them and help them when necessary. You will soon realize that our children are more capable of solving their own problems than we ever imagined. It is as easy as starting with making a clear request.

I listen to a lot of complaints in my office. None of which are productive. Only when someone says to me, "This is what I need or want," do we start to get somewhere. Otherwise, neither of us knows what to do!

CHAPTER 24

# No Prom for Me

As my high school senior approaches graduation, I realize that there is another problem with our society apart from parents who enable their children. We lack compassion.

We have senior breakfasts, senior proms, senior parties. Rarely does the administration of a school consider how to help those children who cannot attend a prom or a school event. We have worked so hard to include intellectually and developmentally delayed children in school events. My heart is warmed by the efforts the schools have made to include my Jackie in chorus and band and theater, but what about the forgotten children? What about the child with chronic anxiety who cannot enter a room filled with people? What about the homebound child who is chronically ill? What about the child who is depressed? Is there nothing we as a society can offer these children to feel a sense of worth and belonging? I have observed these families and many are just relieved to be done with high school. I believe these children deserve a celebration beyond a sigh of relief. But how?

The lack of compassion is also found in other parents who continually ask the question, "Where your child is going to college?" (At least this is the norm, in my neck of the woods. Feel free to replace the question with "What is your kid going to do after high school?" if college is not the norm for you.) So this goes out to those parents who have children who will never attend a school dance or maybe not even be able to attend their own graduation due to disabilities or anxiety. I told my son he had to participate in the graduation ceremony, because I deserved it for all of my efforts over the last 18 years! He tried so hard to enjoy himself. He put on a good show despite barely tolerating the endless ceremony and a hat that almost drove him to run out of the building.

Every time I hear another parent talking about their child heading off to college, my heart hurts. My son, even though he was accepted into a good school and received a scholarship, is unable to go to college and live independently. He has no desire to participate in school activities. The thought of him going to prom is almost a joke. The noise, the chaos, the crowd, none of it appeals to him. I'm lucky to get him to go to a family party, and even then, he persistently asks when we are going home.

For those families with children who do not fit the mold, my heart is with you. You may never get the privilege of watching your child play a sport or go off on a date or to a basketball game at the high school. For every parent who has the opportunity of watching their child do any of these things, I pray you bask in gratitude for these moments that are so easy to take for granted. Be amazed that your child can learn to read with ease. Consider the miracle of the brain coordinating with the body so your child can play a sport or feed themselves or play without pain. Tuck these moments into a safe place in your heart; they will carry you through those times when the very same kid is driving you crazy.

I took a walk with my littlest child and saw groups of teenagers dressed for prom having their pictures taken by proud parents. All I felt was pain. This is not what I dreamed of the first time I held my baby boy. I envisioned such a bright future for him. I pictured him getting his driver's license, his first date, going out with friends, going off to college. I just read Rob Lowe's book *Love Life*. I really admire Mr. Lowe and his enlightened path. I was touched by his description of the emotional roller coaster of watching one's child leave home for college. I wonder, though, what is more painful—watching your child go off to start their own life, or knowing that your child will not be capable of going off to live on their own? That is a pain that is indescribable. There is fear, anger, shame, and panic all rolled into a ball that encompasses your heart to the point where it is hard to breathe.

I have no easy answer for this one. Maybe, breathe? Maybe, faith?

What I do know is we must as parents stop comparing our children's experience to others. Wishing for a prom experience that would torture your child is your pain, not your child's. Try to look at the world through your child's eyes. Are they really missing out by not participating in sports, extracurricular events or parties? If the answer is no, let it go. Watch for what resonates with your child. What makes them laugh? When are they happy? Where are they content? How do they want to be seen?

When we shift our focus to the child rather than our pain, a new world opens up. A world we may or may not be familiar with. I hear joy in Joey's voice when he is online gaming with his group of friends, some of whom are across the globe. He is funny, engaged and smiling. This is his world, his joy. He loves to learn about politics and world events. He is witty and kind beyond measure, and he cannot tolerate car rides, vacations or loud events. I need to allow Joey to find his way in the world without judging his experience. Just as he thinks I'm crazy for spending hours wandering through antique stores, I need to honor his way of engaging in the world. It is then I can let go of my disappointments and grief and celebrate the unique young man standing in front of me, no matter how alien his experience may seem to me. I can be compassionate to him and to others.

CHAPTER 25

# I Don't Deserve This!

If you have a child in a situation similar to what I just described, you might resonate with the sentence: I don't deserve this.

If you find yourself one day, as I often do, saying to yourself and anyone within earshot, "I don't deserve this!"—please, stop. Breathe. Breathe for a couple more hours.

This feeling is a sign. A sign that you are stuck in something. It's an opportunity to break an unhealthy pattern (probably a self-limiting belief). So when I get the call from the middle school that my 13-year-old daughter is serving after school detention for hiding in the bathroom because she hates PE for five days in a row (how she pulled that off is a testament to her intelligence), then I get the email saying my youngest has become angry and defiant at school (probably due to a new medicine I put her on hoping to calm her brutal anxiety), and my oldest son is refusing to write in-class essays despite endless support, and my 15-year-old is screaming at me that it is my job to make him feel better and help him with his homework at 11:00 p.m., and I'm thinking I don't deserve this...I need to stop and breathe.

Life is unpredictable. Your expectation that your life should be happy and easy will cause you pain. When you ask people who have lived very difficult lives, who have survived and thrived (think Oprah), they will say they would not change a thing because they would not be the person they are today without the lessons they learned along the way. Lessons are meant to be challenging and, yes, sometimes ugly. Those are the ones we never forget.

So my lesson in this particular moment, when I screamed through tears, "I don't deserve this!" was…I can't control this. When I calmed after the emotional collapse and released my desire for control, it all stopped. Literally.

It is a beautiful day when you realize the best metaphor for life is a hurricane. You can find peace in the center of uncontrollable chaos. And the hurricane will pass. Again, there is that gift of time.

I was stuck in my need for control in the midst of a storm I would never control in a million years. If I release my need to control everything, I can calm my fear and find my wise, grounded self. I am smart and resourceful. I can handle anything. It might be emotionally brutal, but I can be okay even with painful emotions. Emotions, like hurricanes, will pass if we let them. You have to experience the emotions for them to pass.

Don't think you're different from the rest of us and do not have a need to feel your emotions. If you think that, you'll experience serious repercussions. It will get ugly, and you will look around one day and wonder why you are even on the planet. What is the point if you are denying yourself the human experience? I'll let you in on a little secret. You cannot experience joy if you do not allow yourself to feel sadness. Joy and sadness are not opposites. You can experience both joy and sadness in the same moment.

You deserve to grow and learn from life. Can you be someone who greets life's challenges with the excitement and joy of being alive in this moment to experience the thrill of being human? What if you invited life's lessons and were grateful? It is like the athlete who looks at that marathon with a rush of adrenalin at the opportunity to conquer it. How well do you think that runner might perform if he was scared to death he was not going to finish? He probably would not. The mind is so powerful. Use it to your advantage.

I kind of envy extreme sports nuts. They love a challenge. They are able to overcome fear because they know they are strong and can handle anything. While I will never jump out of a plane or ride a motorcycle or snowboard the half-pipe, I will see a challenge coming in life and face it with enthusiasm as another opportunity to learn something and evolve as an enlightened being. I will come out wiser and stronger on the other side. While I still flip off the universe in moments that are really tough, I always return to gratitude. My children are my greatest teachers who are master lesson planners. They have come up with some of my best learning moments. I equate life's problems to going to the gym to work out. The workout might be hard and unpleasant, however afterwards I feel good about myself, and I am healthier for it.

I now follow every scream of "I don't deserve this!" with a prayer of gratitude for the free workout.

CHAPTER 26

# Really? I Have to Deal With This, Too?

It's hard enough coping with children who have disabilities or are keeping the psychiatric profession thriving. It's like living under a magnifying glass. Life starts to get so hot that all your issues get triggered all of the time. You either break down, seek therapeutic or psychiatric help yourself, or you end up messing up everyone around you including yourself. This is why so many relationships are torn apart when they have a child with special needs. Without having extraordinary self-awareness and lots of tools for handling conflict, it's a rare relationship that can survive the intense challenges of parenting a child with extraordinary needs. It's like living in a pressure cooker. Mom is fried from grief, stress and worry. She is desperately trying to help, finding specialist after specialist. Dad is scared to death and just agrees with everything mom says or challenges every decision based on the price tag (the only logical thing he can bring to the table because the emotions are not accessible or they are overwhelming). Mom becomes resentful because she feels like she is carrying the weight of the life of this child alone. And anything, any disagreement, is likely to throw a match on a dry haystack covered in gasoline.

So the cherry on the cake is when some relative or friend or just some person with no filter comes to you with "All you need to do is…."

"Thank you! I had not tried that. In fact, I am so unbelievably stupid, I never even thought of it!" Sometimes they even have the gall to throw in, "Look at my kids, they're doing great!"

I've got news for you. Children are independent beings. They have their unique genetic coding and brain structure. They have their own personalities and lessons to learn. The way each person goes about learning his or her lessons is highly unique. We must honor the path our children are on as their own. For those parents who feel the weight of their child's lives, put it down.

I hate it when people feel sorry for me because I'm dyslexic, epileptic, physically challenged by a genetic disorder, or in pain. I don't want people's pity or even their empathy. I want people to look at me as a wholly capable person completely able to handle her own difficulties. In fact, I get a bit feisty when people underestimate me, for whatever reason, and become driven by an intense need to prove to everyone that I am highly capable and, dare I say, pretty intelligent in my own ways. As a kid I never thought for a second it was my parent's job to fix my difficulties or me.

Your kids, no matter what challenges or quirks they may be blessed with, do not want you to carry them. They want to be seen as capable and resourceful with no need for change, just as they are. And the only way a parent can see their child that way is by letting go and putting down the life that was not theirs to carry in the first place. Love them, teach them, be a model for them, support them, and never take their power away. If you stop believing them capable, you disempower them, and they quickly believe they are not okay as they are. Their self-esteem becomes subject to doubt because if your own parents do not believe you are capable then why should you believe it?

I have seen too many parents open themselves up to serious psychiatric problems, depression, anxiety, panic disorder and codependency, because they took on the full emotional weight of their child's struggle. The sad part is none of the parent's suffering actually helped the child at all. In fact, the parent's suffering only worsens the child's condition. Given we are empathic creatures who sense the feelings and conditions of those around us, we are deeply affected by the depression or worry of a loved one. For a child, adding to their already complex lives, worrying about their parents is extremely difficult.

You had this experience as a kid: you sensed when your dad was really pissed about something and you avoided him like the plague. As an adult, you know within seconds upon entering a room that something is going on. It could be at school, work or home. You don't need someone to explain that something is up. You feel it. People do not need to exchange words to sense something is afoot.

Animals are incredibly gifted at sensing emotions and energetic changes in humans. Every wonder why your cat crawls into your lap just when you need her to, or why your dog follows your sick child like a concerned mother? My son's psychologist has a trained dog in her office named Charlie. For whatever reason, Charlie jumps into Joey's lap and licks him to death during his sessions. Joe seems to like it whereas someone else might become annoyed. Charlie knows she is calming Joey's untouchable anxiety. If only Charlie could tell us what she knows about Joey and his seemingly untreatable condition. I bet Charlie knows quite a bit.

While we may not have the emotional or energetic radar some animals do, we do have radar. You know someone's general state without them telling you. I know when my husband is upset. He (unfortunately) knows every thought that runs through my head whether I want him to or not. There are obvious signs of body posture, facial expressions, expressed emotions, but even when I am putting up a good front or a stiff upper lip, he still knows. How many of you moms out there had the experience of your mother telling you she knew you were pregnant before you knew yourself?

Our children sense our worry, concern, depression, anxiety and stress. It adds to their load because you are their lifeline, their compass, their supposed rock. Do them a favor and take care of yourself—if not for yourself, then for your child whom you love. Go get help, exercise, eat well, meditate, sleep and process your emotions in a healthy way. And give your child the greatest gift you can give them, the best version of you who sees them as the miraculous, god-like creatures they really are. Perfect with no need for change. They will sense it and amazing things will happen. And when they do, send me your story. My life's purpose will then be fulfilled.

Honor your child's struggle as you would want someone to honor yours. Every life is important no matter the circumstance. They all serve a purpose. Ours is not to judge others or ourselves. Our purpose is to grow in wisdom and to love. If you make that your purpose in life, you will have your answer. Love, joy, fulfillment, peace, strength, it will all be yours.

And, ignore anyone who is giving you advice that is serving their own ego.

CHAPTER 27

# Better Off Dead

Not only do we have to deal with the judgments of others, we have to deal with the endless conversation in our own head. This conversation can be even more damaging than the ones we have with other people. We are hard on ourselves.

Do you ever consider, "Would they all be better off if I were dead?"

Not to be morbid, just honest. This needs to be brought out into the light. I think this thought quite often. When your child is not thriving, the temptation is to fantasize that you are to blame. Someone else would have handled this with more grace, made better decisions, and had more success.

But you know this child would have some serious grief to deal with if you up and disappeared. Why would you add to their problems by forcing them to lose the parent who loves them so dearly? You would not.

So why are you torturing your heart with a lie you do not even believe? You are trying to find words that reflect the actual intensity of your emotions. You are in pain, suffering, afraid, uncertain. You have given yourself away, and you are exhausted. You have abandoned yourself, your needs, your emotional health, and probably your physical health.

Let's try together to find a healthier way to express your emotions, which are incredibly complex. What if you were to say, "I am exhausted. I need to rest. I don't know how to rest when my child's needs are so demanding. I fear others will judge me a bad parent, and I cannot bear that shame. How can it be okay to put my needs before those of others?"

"I am terrified that I won't be okay if my child does not need me." This was my true fear. I had my identity so wrapped up in my oldest son, I was constantly anxious and stressed no matter how well or poorly he was doing.

"I am resentful I have to deal with this." Many parents who have unique children feel all alone. They are so angry they cannot even recognize it when someone is trying to be supportive.

"I feel guilty for wishing my child was normal (whatever that looks like)," or "I feel guilty for wishing I did not have children." I often wonder what do people without children do all day? It must be lovely taking regular showers, eating proper meals, catching up on world events, seeing movies, reading books, relaxing, exercising, and spending time with friends.

Look into the eyes of a woman or man who was unable to conceive a child or who has lost a child. They would trade places with you in a heartbeat. The grass is not always greener.

Children are a gift. We must focus on gratitude. Ask, "What have I learned from these children?" I do not have enough years left in this lifetime to even come close to sharing what I have learned from my children.

I may struggle with my normal emotions of anger, fear, resentment, jealousy, shame, grief, loneliness and hopelessness, but when I am still, I feel warmth in my heart that reminds me: this is all as it should be. No matter the chaos in one's life, whether it be a struggling or sick child, a dying parent or financial ruin, addiction, fear, death, grief, or anxiety, the only thing that matters, the only thing that will maintain your sanity, your sense of fulfillment in life, is your ability to find your true self. You will find your heart, your identity, and walk your own path with love, knowing that you are loved and important. You are human and learning and growing until your body dies.

Love yourself. My greatest moment of relief came when I stopped looking for the love I felt in my heart to come from other people. When I allowed myself to bask in the warmth of my own self-love, my expectations and disappointment in others melted away, and I felt strong and whole for the first time ever.

It is your choice whether you take this journey filled with love and gratitude for all the challenges you faced, or you choose to kick and scream and complain and refuse to address your own humanity and the emotions that come along with it. Either way, the chaos, the things over which you have absolutely no control (e.g. being born into poverty or disability) will not be affected by your state. Hurricanes happen. Life gets messy. When you find yourself in a hurricane, move to the eye of the storm. There you will find peace and clarity. At the eye of the storm are your heart, your true self, and your wisdom.

We all have our own strategies to find our center. I meditate. I practice forgiveness to others and to myself. I ask for forgiveness when necessary.

My children would not be better off with a different mom. They love me, and I love them. They learn from me including my mistakes and how I handle them, hopefully with grace, and I learn from my children, over and over and over again. The universe is relentless that way. I allow my emotions, I honor them, I am grateful for their messages, and then I release them. I continue to love, even myself. I feel this is the hardest love of all to master, self-love. Life may be chaos, but it is as it should be, perfect, with no need for change.

In this state, I am present for all the wonderful, joyful moments. The hug from Jackie. The feeling that she is loving me, patting my back, saying, "It's okay, honey." The enthusiasm for knowledge emanating from Kelly. Her huge heart and her crocodile tears from those big, beautiful eyes that are pure magic. Tommy's amazing talent, his unbelievable empathy, his silly nature that makes me laugh and just love life. Joey's fantastic, dry wit. His ability to be funny and brilliant in one small profound sentence. His resilience and extraordinary patience with children and his sisters. My children are kind, loving people at their core. They are independent thinkers and leaders in their own ways. I would hate to miss a second of it, even the most painful ones.

It is my choice how to perceive my children and our journey together. I have chosen fear in moments. I do not like it, and I do not recommend it. I have learned to use fear as my teacher to help me find my way back to love. I then can heal my wounds and feel strong. It is then I can be a good parent to my children.

CHAPTER 28

# The Ramen Noodle Conundrum

You may think other people's words do not bother you. You may even believe you have mastered your own mind. (I am skeptical about that.) However, no one has mastered the mighty teenager. The teen years are a comin'. You know this. You prepare yourself for the tsunami everyone talks about. So, why do we get so triggered by our teens?

I hear this all the time. "My teenager drives me crazy!" Why? Why do we go nuts when our teen argues with us for the sake of disagreeing? When they push us away or refuse our wisdom and attempt to reinvent their own, we are livid. What would happen to society if all teens were drugged into a subservient mindset?

I tell you what. They would never leave the comfort of home. Universities everywhere would go out of business. Think about what drove you to leave home. Was it the home-cooked meals? The laundry service? The cozy bed?

No, you probably could not stand the thought of not going out into the world and creating your own life with your own friends. You wanted to be with people your own age and share ideas, find friends and people to have sex with and to love.

Think of evolution. How would societies evolve if teenagers were not crazy enough to leave the cozy life of home (if they are lucky enough to be in that situation) and live in debt or struggle for enough money to eat out beyond Taco Bell? I chose Ramen noodles over my mom's beautifully prepared dinners. Why? Was I masochistic? No. I was a teenager pushing away from home to create a life with those of my generation that was more evolved than that of my parents.

So if we know it is coming, why do we get so triggered by normal human behavior? When my teenage boy starts to have an irrational argument with me, I have a choice. I could argue back spiraling the house into WWIII. Or, I could choose to honor his anger, frustration, or hurt, and support him through his difficult moment, which may look like removing myself from the argument completely.

It is no different when you have a baby who is colicky or who refuses to sleep at night no matter how much you comfort them. You knew this was a possibility. So, while it may be unpleasant, you do not say, "Those damn babies these days! They are so self-centered!"

Teenagers offer us an opportunity to grow as a society because they are determined to go off and find a better way. Thank goodness! The world needs a lot of improvement.

Choose wisely. You can be the model of sanity and rationality for them during their formative years of adolescence, or you can completely discredit yourself by reacting to their impulsivity and engaging in their arguments.

So set and hold your wise, loving boundaries to keep them safe and be thrilled your 13-year-old is seeking her own form of self-expression. Green hair for a couple of months is nothing compared to the heartache of watching your older teen be so crippled by anxiety that they cannot leave home.

Prepare yourself for these developmental phases. If you know you cannot stand people who test the limits of authority, go internal and find out why. Get help from a therapist or spiritual leader. The problem is in you, not in your son's desire to stay out after curfew. He is normal; your insane reaction is not. Having firmly agreed upon consequences is normal. Chewing the kid out when they are late is not.

I personally cannot stand it when my kids blame me for their emotional pain. Like it's really my ill intent at play when I choose to take one to the psychologist and therefore cannot drive the other to his girlfriend's house. (Either way I'm not having any fun.) My other trigger is when they suddenly realize they need my help with homework as I am climbing the stairs to go to bed exhausted at 11:00 p.m. If I say, "No, you should have asked me earlier, maybe during the three hour window in which you were playing Dota online," I get the whiny response, "But Moooommmm! You never help me, and it will be your fault if I get an F on this assignment."

Really? How does that logic hold water? I just did your laundry, made you multiple meals that were completely different than what everyone else was eating, picked up your stuff, and offered to help you around 6:00 p.m. with homework which you refused because you did not "think" you had any homework. How convenient. No matter how you come at this beast, they will point the mighty finger of blame in your direction.

It's your job to grab that finger and turn it in their direction. Do not take on any of the guilt or negative energy they are trying to throw your way. If you cave even a little they will sense it like a shark can sense a single drop of blood in the water a mile away. They will circle you waiting for you to weaken and eventually consume you and all your energy. They are predators. You need to not show any fear, or they will sense it and go in for the kill. I kid you not. They will find your weakness and play it like a skilled musician. Kids know your triggers, what sets you off, and your shame. They will find a way to break you, if you let them. It is their instinct.

So, here is the key to this one. Be a rock. Literally. You have to hold that boundary as if it were a front line in WWII. Any sign there is a gap in that line, the enemy will go right for it. Now, many parents will argue that they hold boundaries "most" of the time. Well, it's like this. If you just give in once with a child, they know that if they push hard enough or whine long enough, they might just get their way. What have they got to lose? It's like gambling.

Neurologically, we all can relate to gamblers, and how addictive gambling can be. You may pull the slot level 1000 times and never win a dime. However! If you win on the 1001st pull, you will get a huge hit of dopamine in your brain, which is like heroin. One shot of it and you may become addicted. Unpredictable rewards for any behavior reinforce that behavior like cement.

You cave once on a boundary and you have just undone maybe months of holding a firm boundary with your child. This is neuroscience at its most enlightening. If you never win when you pull the slot machine arm, you will eventually give up. It may take a couple of trips to the casino, and you may lose hundreds if not thousands of dollars before you decide there is no dopamine to be found there. If a child knows that you will never allow them to eat cookies before dinner, eventually they will stop asking. If you allow it once, you have created a crazed gambler looking for his next big score.

So stand firm no matter what emotions come up for you. It will make your life much easier in the long run. Go off and deal with your emotions away from your child. Get help if necessary. I do.

And remember, it is normal for teenagers to test boundaries, just like toddlers. They will try stupid things and push you away. That's normal. You can hold your safety boundaries (e.g. under no circumstances will you drive the car after the local curfew). You can hold your respect boundaries (e.g. under no circumstances are you to yell or curse at me).

Accept procrastination, immediate gratification, lack of planning, and not considering consequences as hallmarks of the developing teenage brain. So what is the issue triggering me into an internal rage, causing me to lose control of my grace and, sometimes, scream like a lunatic when my teenager is being a teenager?

The answer lies in my desire for control and perfection because I believe/believed that control and perfection were critical ingredients for feeling okay. I believed as a child I was unlovable unless I was perfect. Sadly, no matter how good I was, I was not experiencing the love I wanted to feel (which was, in actuality, love for myself). I was too young to understand what I was seeking. This drove me to try harder, creating a fear of failure to the point that the slightest criticism was interpreted as a threat to my very existence. So, my children telling me or even hinting I was causing them emotional turmoil triggered my core shame. I was being imperfect. A perfect mother would never cause their children pain. Everyone should be happy in a perfect world. I was also projecting my desire for control and perfection onto my children. It sounds ridiculous when you see it on paper, but this is my truth. I bet your truth is not too different from mine.

When I went and worked on understanding the origin of my shame issues, I no longer reacted to my children's criticisms. My expectations of them became more realistic. I stopped taking everything so personally. And in moments when I do react (because I am human), I am wise enough to step away to calm myself before I go any further. If I do lose it, I clean it up later.

So when your teenagers choose Ramen noodles over you, celebrate they are doing exactly what they should be doing: creating their own life.

CHAPTER 29

# What Should We Be Teaching Our Children?

Sports are fun. Music lessons are great. Good grades open doors. Valuing money will make life easier. Serious conversations about drugs and sex are important. But I believe today, most of us are missing the boat on parenting.

First, we need to love our children unconditionally. This is not easy. Can you unconditionally shower your child with love if they're a drug addict, a criminal, a high school dropout, a psychiatric mess, crippled or chronically ill? Be honest. It is difficult to give love freely when we feel vulnerable. The child may not be capable of returning our love. We may be stuck in our own judgment. We may fear we may not be okay if the child dies or does not live up to our arbitrarily set expectations, so we protect our hearts.

To give love freely without conditions (e.g. I must be loved in return) or without judgment (e.g. I will love you as long as you live within my own moral code of comfort) is the most powerful feeling one can experience.

It seems so simple, yet few humans have ever reached such nirvana. I have felt it in moments, and as I grow stronger and wiser, I bask in the strength of this unconditional love more and more. I feel free, free of the burdens that should be carried by others, even my children. And miraculously, the people I love unconditionally feel it and are empowered. What a gift to know that someone out there loves you, no matter what your flaws may be.

I have felt this love, given by my enlightened friends, my husband and by my children. Children love unconditionally until they unlearn.

Be the model of unconditional love for your children. They will learn by watching you. You will stop judging others and stop separating humans into groups by whatever means: race, color, sexual orientation, gender, age, ability, intellect. We are all human. That is all that matters. Be the person you want your children to become. Be kind. Accept everyone just as they are. You do not have to invite them to dinner, just accept who they are and do not judge them. Forgive and ask for forgiveness. Be fully present for those you love. Be generous. Feel abundant. Most important, love yourself.

Look in the mirror and love yourself. If you cannot, ask yourself why and work to let that reason go. This may require help, and that is as it should be because we were never meant to go it alone. Whoever came up with the notion that independence is such a good thing forgot we are social beings. We are meant to help each other.

Love yourself because you are lovable and deserve love. Love yourself because you want to teach your children to love themselves.

Parenting will then become the joy it was meant to be.

# Appendix

## Book References

*The Book of Forgiving: The Fourfold Path for Healing Ourselves and Our World* by Desmond and Mpho Tutu

*Buddha's Brain: Happiness, Love & Wisdom* by Rick Hanson, PhD and Richard Mendius, MD

*Connected: The Surprising Power of Our Social Networks and How They Shape Our Lives* by Dr. Nicholas A. Chirstakis and Dr. James H. Fowler

*The Whole-Brain Child* by Dr. Daniel Siegel and Dr. Tina Payne Bryson

Made in the USA
Lexington, KY
12 June 2017